spirituality
in
interfaith
dialogue

spirituality
in
interfaith
dialogue

Edited by Tosh Arai
and Wesley Ariarajah

ORBIS BOOKS

Maryknoll, New York 10545

The Catholic Foreign Mission Society of America (Maryknoll) recruits and trains people for overseas missionary service. Through Orbis Books, Maryknoll aims to foster the international dialogue that is essential to mission. The books published, however, reflect the opinions of their authors and are not meant to represent the official position of the society.

ORBIS/ISBN 0-88344-524-7

Table of Contents

Introduction   vii

Statement   1

Listening to the Silence: Through Zen and Taizé, *by Michael Como*   3

Discovering the Incarnation, *by Diana Eck*   8

On the Pilgrim Path, *by C. Murray Rogers*   13

Journey Towards an Inclusive Spirituality,
by M. Thomas Thangaraj   19

In Search of Being one with the One, *by Mataji Vandana*   23

Interiority, Awareness and Realization, *by Swami Amaldas*   31

A Journey with the Unknown, *by Bettina Bäumer*   36

Beyond Words and Logic, *by Chewn Jiuan A. Lee*   42

Through Other Religious Disciplines   45

   Learning to Let Go, *by Pascaline Coff, OSB*   45

   Enlightenment through Zen, *by Thomas G. Hand, SJ*   49

   A Search for Spiritual Roots, *by Peter K.H. Lee*   53

The World of Spiritual Discoveries, *by Mary O. Driscoll, OP* . . .   60

Living Dialogue, *by Yohan Devananda*   67

Experience of Spirituality in Dialogue, *by John C. England*   78

Deepening our Understanding of Spirituality, *by Yves Raguin, SJ* .   81

From Diverse Situations   87

  Oneness at the Centre, *by Khalil Zomkhol*   87

  Journey through the Gateless Gate, *by Hakan Eilert*   91

  Integrating Other Religious Traditions
  into Western Christianity, *by Arnold Bittlinger*   96

  Exploring Aboriginal Spirituality, *by Colin Alcock*   101

Introduction

"Spirituality in Interfaith Dialogue" was the theme of a consultation which met at the Kansai Seminar House, Kyoto, Japan, from 1 to 5 December 1987. The consultation was jointly sponsored by the World Council of Churches' Sub-units on Renewal and Congregational Life (RCL) and on Dialogue with People of Living Faiths.

One of RCL's major concerns since the Vancouver Assembly of the WCC in 1983 has been the exploration of "a spirituality for our times". The dialogue of spiritualities has through the years received the attention also of the Dialogue Sub-unit. The theme of the consultation thus represented an area of interest for both sub-units, an area where their work in a real sense coalesced.

The consultation brought together people belonging to Roman Catholic, Orthodox and Protestant traditions, men and women who had for years lived in dialogue with people of other faiths and, in many instances, shared in depth in the spiritualities of these faiths. Its purpose was to explore what such dialogue with and sharing in the spiritualities of other traditions have meant to them personally and to find out whether what they have learned and gained could contribute to the life of ordinary Christians, both as individuals and congregations.

The consultation addressed itself to questions like these:

What individual spiritual journeys have led Christians into the spiritual life of other religious traditions? What problems have they encountered in this pursuit, and what insights and perspectives have they gained?

What kinds of mutual enrichment have they found in spiritual dialogue with people of other faiths? What have they discovered in the traditions of the other? What have they rediscovered in their own tradition?

How may such discoveries and insights renew and enrich the life of our congregations and Christians in general? Why are many of our churches hesitant or cautious about sharing in the spirituality of other people? What can be done to overcome such cautiousness?

What are the theological and pastoral issues involved?

The first two days of the meeting were devoted to the sharing of experiences. A number of participants had for years immersed themselves in Buddhist and Hindu spiritualities followed their ancient disciplines. One of the participants invariably referred to herself as a Hindu Catholic. Quite a few had for considerable periods lived in Zen monasteries and Hindu ashrams. A few had been involved in the struggles of the poor and in movements of development and liberation.

The account of their spiritual pilgrimages was a rich dialogue in itself, and perhaps the most rewarding part of the consultation.

But do such experiences, born out of individual journeys for the most part and consisting largely of experiments in the discipline of interiority, lend themselves to be transferred? Can they contribute to the spiritual formation of congregations?

Participants affirmed the plurality of spiritualities. Where such plurality is evident in the life of a congregation, it needs to be cherished and encouraged. Also emphasized was the need to draw up and implement programmes of biblical and theological education for members of congregations, for spiritual renewal can only happen through people. Yet another emphasis was on the need to provide for meaningful exposures to other spiritualities.

A good deal of time was spent in group discussions. Participants were divided into three groups, each focusing on a specific question.

The first group explored ways to enable Christians and congregations to benefit through being open to the experiences of other spiritual traditions. Members of the group suspected that for many of their fellow Christians the question did not arise; for them their own faith was all-sufficient, and they had little inclination to explore other spiritual traditions. But all the members of the group testified from their personal experience that the exposure to other spiritual disciplines enabled them to understand their own faith at greater depth. It gave them the conviction that God was at work in the whole world, not just in the Christian part of it, and that they belonged to the larger human family. For some it had opened up the Bible in new ways. An Indian Christian participant affirmed that the exploration of Hinduism had given him a new sense of identity; he was also convinced that the massive problems facing his country could not be tackled in isolation from other religious communities.

The group identified teaching and exposure as the two major ways of helping people towards an appreciation of other spiritualities. Thus there is the need to develop a new hermeneutics and a new exegetical tradition of the Bible which would take plurality more seriously. The "exclusivistic" texts of the Bible should receive greater attention; far too often they are used divisively and judgmentally. It is also necessary to reread the Bible putting people at the centre, and to explicate more fully the teaching about the cosmic Christ.

The group recommended the holding of planned meetings to promote friendship between people and exchange of ideas. Multifaith study groups could deal with specific issues of faith and of life together in community. Common action in terms of conflict and tension can be a strong witness. People may take part in the festivals of other communities and study the meaning of the rituals and symbols they have seen.

In situations where Christians and congregations are open to or are already exposed to other spiritual disciplines, what help may be given to them to understand and appropriate them in the context of their Christian faith? That was the question discussed by the second group. Members recommended the use of a variety of devotional resources. Among the books mentioned were Raymond Panikkar's *Vedic Experience*, Sara Grant's booklet on Upanishadic and biblical texts, Bettina Bäumer's volumes (in German) on Indian spirituality, Kadawaki's *Zen and the Bible* and the Archbishop of Canterbury's *Progress for Peace*. There is need perhaps to make available to people a carefully chosen book of scriptural readings and prayers from various spiritual traditions.

It is important for Christians to prepare themselves before they are exposed to the riches of other traditions. We must get to know the writings of our own mystics and saints and deepen our own practices of devotion. We need to be in dialogue with fellow Christians on matters spiritual and on the plurality of Christian spiritualities and artistic expressions.

Members suggested the starting of study groups in parishes, the conducting of yoga or zen sessions over a period of weeks, and sharing with friends of other communities in their religious celebrations. They were concerned over the fear, especially in Western countries, of the "invasion" of oriental religions. It is not always easy to distinguish between authentic and pseudo spiritual movements, and the ecumenical community has the responsibility to help people in the discerning of the spirits.

The third group addressed the question: What are the ways to enable Christians and congregations to engage with people of other religious traditions in the struggles in society? How do we help them towards the understanding that such engagement is an expression of spirituality? The report of the group says:

We first took note of the dire conditions of poverty, oppression and suffering in which vast numbers of people in the world live, especially in the third world. The call to engage with them in their just struggles for a more humane way of life is a call, at the same time, to stand by Christ in his work among them, working for change and transformation with them.

We then shared the experiences of the members of our group in engagement in the struggles in society. They were stories of the engagement of church groups, church-related groups, and interfaith as well as interfaith and inter-ideological groups. We heard stories from New Zealand, South Africa, Japan, Hong Kong, Sri Lanka and India. These were stories of struggle for minority rights, human rights, land rights of peasants, rights of the workers and urban poor and of depressed castes, women's rights, peace movements and stories of opposition to nuclear weapons and militarization, multi-nationals, etc. A notable feature of Christian participation in such struggles is that it is not only those who are known as radical Christians who are engaged in them but also those who are known as strong evangelicals. Specific instances were given of the latter from revivalist and reform movements in the USA and from liberation movements in South Korea and the Philippines. That is, when repressive conditions in society become unbearable the people rise up whether they are "radicals" or "evangelicals".

There is indeed a clear movement throughout the world for development, justice and liberation in which people of living faiths and ideologies are already becoming involved. However, the need for more positive and effective involvement is clear and urgent. How can this be carried further and deeper?

Bishops, clergy and lay leaders of the churches, wherever possible in cooperation with leaders of other living faiths and ideologies, can respond by taking a stand, speaking up for and supporting movements of development, justice and liberation. They can encourage the engagement of their peoples in the struggles of society in various ways. Exposure programmes could be increasingly promoted. Groups could visit various situations of oppression and suffering among workers and peasants, depressed castes, refugees, minorities, etc. Alternatively, groups or leaders from these situations could be invited to visit church groups (that is, both going out for exposure, as well as bringing others in to us). Another creative possibility which has been sometimes tried out but could be increasingly used is the organizing of seminars, youth camps, work camps, etc. on an interfaith basis.

It is being increasingly recognized by Christians as well as those of other living faiths and ideologies that such engagement should lead not only to attempts to relieve the poor but support them in a more fundamental way. In other words, not merely social service in the limited sense is called for but social action. The themes of development, justice and liberation have to be explored in their deeper and wider senses, in a movement of action-reflection. The causes of poverty and oppression and the resources and methods for change and transformation have to be researched, analyzed and studied. This is sometimes referred to as a movement or process of conscientization or revolution of mind and spirit.

As people become engaged in this they will be able to discover such an engagement as an expression of true spirituality. The Bible as well as other scriptures and texts will come alive as they are read with new eyes. There is also an increasing number of books, journals and articles that have come out of such engagement which will help those who wish to explore further.

Statement

We who have come to this consultation — Orthodox, Catholic, Protestant — have shared our individual spiritual journeys as Christians who, in a variety of ways, have been nourished and enriched by the spiritual life of our neighbours of other faiths. What has motivated us in our journeys? What have been the struggles along the way? What insights and perspectives have we gained? In what ways have we rediscovered our own spiritual traditions through such exchange and dialogue? How might such experience be shared in our communal and congregational life as Christians? These were the questions we explored in our week together.

We come from many different contexts. Some of us, especially those of us from Asia, have been motivated in our journey by the search for a spirituality that is authentic and meaningful in our own cultural context. This has raised for us the question of how we might appreciate the spiritual disciplines, the prayers and the scriptures of our neighbours, and the artistic or musical traditions of the culture we share with our neighbours. Others among us, including many from the West, have been motivated in our spiritual journey by a sense that there was "something missing" in the spiritual life of our own churches, a shallowness, or emptiness, or lack of deepening guidance. In the Hindu and Buddhist traditions especially, we have found forms of practice and prayer that have been both challenging and enriching. For some, it was reading a book such as the *Tao Te Ching* or experiencing the worship of Hindu friends that seized us and moved us to look more deeply. For those of us who are monastics, it has been the dialogue with brothers and sisters in other contemplative traditions that has motivated our journey. And for those of us involved in social action programmes, it has been in the very work of joining hands with people of other faiths in the struggle for a new society that we have been spiritually renewed.

Sharing our stories and journeys and reflecting on them together, we have sensed among us some common affirmations. First, we affirm the great value of dialogue at the level of spirituality in coming to know and understand people of other faiths as people of prayer and spiritual practice, as seekers and pilgrims with us, and as partners with us in working for peace and justice. Second, we affirm the deepening of our own Christian faith in the journeys that have taken us into the spiritual life and practice of other faiths. In walking along with the other, with the stranger, like the disciples on the road to Emmaus, we have had, in our sharing, the experience of recognition. We have seen the unexpected Christ and have been renewed. Third, we affirm the work of the Spirit in ways that move beyond the Christian compound and across the frontiers of religion and takes us into creative involvement with people of other faiths in the struggles of the world.

What might such affirmations of the spiritual dimensions of dialogue mean for churches and congregations? We have come as individuals although we belong to Christian confessional traditions, and have been honest and open with one another about our own experience. And yet we sense that the questioning and questing that has moved us into spiritual dialogue and exchange is shared by many Christians.

Listening to the Silence: Through Zen and Taizé

MICHAEL COMO

It was meant as a consultation on spirituality. But to many of the participants the consultation itself proved to be a spiritual journey. People who have struggled for years with their spiritual life told their stories with remarkable openness. We begin with the account given by Michael Como, the youngest member of the group.

There's nothing I want to point to and say: "*That's* my Christian practice. The rest you can just forget about." Also, I still am not sure what all the effects of my encounter with another religious tradition have been. It is always easy to assume that people clearly understand how events have affected them and how they feel about what they have experienced. For me at least that has seldom been the case. I will try to set down some of the results which have been easiest for me to see and hope that those seeds still bearing fruit will come to light later.

I guess to begin at the beginning I should say that I was brought up in the United Methodist Church, and attended Sunday school and church services fairly regularly through high school. By the time I went to college, however, I was dissatisfied with almost all of what I had been taught at church — the Christianity which I found dangerously close to simply an exhortation to try and be good if it wasn't too much trouble. There was little sense of struggle or purpose in my church — it felt very far removed from any really pressing questions or issues. What talk there was of God and Jesus simply did not seem credible or, even worse, particularly relevant to anything in my life. It could comfortably be discarded without disturbing my internal equilibrium.

During my first semester at college, however, my outlook on religion changed after reading the *Tao Te Ching* of Lao Tzu. The book had a tremendous impact on me even though I could understand very little of what it said. Soon I wanted to learn everything I could about Asian religions. I became intrigued first by Indian, then by Chinese and Japanese Buddhism. In the place of talk of God, eternity, and the soul, I was attracted to the Buddhist ideals of no-self, impermanence and the co-dependent nature of all things. Impermanence was something easy to believe in, interdependence was its fruit. I felt I no longer needed to seek for a philosophical grounding for the soul or for a way to believe in God without abandoning my intellectual integrity.

I started meditating. My understanding of meditation was very meagre at the time — I saw it mainly as a way of relaxing the body and training the mind. But I gradually realized that it could be more. Personally as well as academically, I felt a need to actually experience the spiritual life about which I had only been reading.

That chance came the summer after my junior year of college. As part of the work on my thesis I lived for three months in the Zen Buddhist monastery of Hosshinji in Obama, Japan. I have never really been able to talk about this experience to my satisfaction. Even three years later, I still do not know what to say, I still am not sure I really understand all that it meant to me.

At Hosshinji I found a community where there was little difference between idea and practice. One monk summarized the Zen way of life with the words "show me!" In other words, "show me what we have learned", "show me the heart of your practice", "show me the Buddha's enlightenment". All that one has learned, he continued, all the blessings one has received are meaningless if they are separated from the concrete activities of one's daily life. As one Zen saying has it, "this very body is Buddha!"

I was very quickly thrown into the heart of this way of life. Three days after I arrived at the monastery there was a *sesshin*, a week of intensive meditation and complete silence. I can still recall how terrified I was and how sore my legs were after the first couple of days. But what surprised me was how good the *sesshin* felt. It was hard, very hard for me, but it was a struggle I realized I had wanted for a long time. It was not a series of irritations, it was a week filled with a sense of purpose and learning.

Day after day I sat with the monks in the meditation hall and, after bowing to my cushion, stared at the partition in front of me. It was beautifully, terrifyingly simple. I didn't have to move or even think; all I had to do was to focus on my breathing. For perhaps the first time in my life I was being asked to do something with my whole self, to simply become centred on the most fundamental act of life.

I couldn't do it. Memories, thoughts, emotions which I had long forgotten, all came back to me as I sat and meditated for thirteen hours each day. I was astonished at how desperately my mind tried to divert itself from the task before me. I saw how in so many ways I was divided within myself. As I found myself growing angry, nostalgic or impatient, the monks told me to simply let go of whatever it was that had come to mind. That week I was forced to confront a lot within me which I would rather not have seen. But in the end I found that I had nowhere to run. I came to accept, to let go of, much of it.

The experience helped me to taste many things which I had previously only thought about. I felt completely free. After each period of meditation I felt so empty, ready to be filled by whatever I met. I just wanted to listen to, to welcome everything around me. It was as if so many obstructions within me had been removed and I was able to relate to things directly for the first time.

The remaining time I spent in the monastery was essentially a deepening and filling out of that first week. The monks were very clear that one must not leave one's Zen in the meditation hall. It must be expressed in, focused on, each new moment and every activity of every day. For perhaps the first time in my life I tried to be truly mindful of whatever I was engaged in. Every moment seemed important, every moment I could start anew. I discovered how beautiful such simple things as a bow, taking a bath, sweeping a garden, could be. There was very little unlived time in the monastery — everything seemed full, ordinary activities seemed special.

Living in the monastery had another, unexpected effect: I became interested in my own Christian heritage. This interest was sparked when one of the monks loaned me a copy of Thomas Merton's *Contemplation in a World of Action*. Not only did the book impress me, it forced me to confront how the life I was leading at Hosshinji related to the Christian monastic tradition. I concluded that the life of meditation and labour that the Hosshinji monks were leading was probably very Christian. The appeal of that life made we want to better understand what Christian contemplative life could be.

My concern with the Christian life intensified after I returned to the States. Readjusting to American society after life in the monastery proved to be very painful and difficult. All around I felt so much separation and violence. I could not integrate what I had learned at Hosshinji with what I was living out in America. I felt that the divisions within me could be healed only by first reconciling myself with my Christian roots. Upon graduating from Harvard, therefore, I went to live at the Protestant monastery of Taizé in France for three months.

At Taizé I found a community at prayer. For years I had not really been able to pray, mainly because I had trouble accepting a God ontologically separated from myself and the world I lived in. After Hosshinji, such a feeling of separation seemed intolerable. I could not open myself to a God who felt so far away. But at Taizé somehow the prayer came first and the understanding later. Simply singing the Taizé liturgy and being a part of the community helped me to feel that I was in a relationship with God, whether I understood it or not.

This feeling of relationship was deepened by a week of silence which I spent under the guidance of one of the brothers. Every day, as I prayed and meditated, I tried to experience the Bible passages I had been assigned. I wanted to live their meaning, I wanted to be able to answer anyone who said "show me!" When I meditated over a psalm of blessing, I wanted to know what it was to praise God. When I was assigned the canticle of Mary, I wanted to really feel what my relationship to her was. The high point of my stay at Taizé came as I sought the answer to this question. As I sat and prayed in the old, medieval church at Taizé, another member of the community came in and also began praying. Suddenly I realized that just as the monks at Hosshinji insisted that each of us was Shakyamuni Buddha in our own bodies, so too could I find Mary in the woman beside me.

After I realized that God and the Christian life could be found within the world and within my own life, my stay at Taizé was transformed. Suddenly I could see the wounds of Christ around me. Suddenly the events in the Bible seemed alive, not simply as moral guidelines, not as theological statements, but as real, continuing events which I could see in my everyday life and in which I could participate.

Today I lead a quiet existence as a junior high school teacher in the small town of Hiraizumi in Northern Japan. My stay here has been peaceful and good. I have needed time to digest all that has happened to me spiritually during the past few years, I have needed a chance to integrate what I have learned with life in secular society. In Hiraizumi I have had that chance. Upon arriving here I first stayed with the family of a Buddhist priest for six months. Every morning we chanted sutras before the Buddha Dainichi, every evening I prayed before my Franciscan cross and an icon of Mary.

Although I now live in my own house, I continue to pray daily before my Japanese-style altar. Upon it, along with the images of Jesus and Mary, is an icon of Shakyamuni Buddha. At times I have tried new approaches to worship; last spring I walked part of the famous Shikoku pilgrimage, last fall I visited the temples and shrines of Nara and Ise. These were very rich, very nourishing experiences; walking along a route travelled by countless pilgrims, praying in temples hundreds of years old, I felt sustained by a tradition not originally my own. Yet at the centre of my practice, quiet though it may be, remains my daily life in this town of 9,000 farmers. Though there is no church here, they have taught me much about human community and love.

As a practice this may seem unremarkable and, in truth, there is probably little that is new or of interest that I can say. But for me it has meant a great deal. I know that for the moment I am where I belong and I trust that I will be led where I need to go when the time comes. That is enough. For the moment I am simply grateful for the life to which I have been awakened to since I was allowed to share in the meditation and communal life of the monks of Hosshinji.

Discovering the Incarnation

DIANA ECK

Deepening and renewing our spiritual life and coming into dialogue with people of other faiths are two of the important concerns of Christians in all parts of the world today. How do these concerns intersect? What are some of the ways in which dialogue might be a source of spiritual renewal? What has it meant for the Christians' own self-understanding? What motivated their journeys? What have been the struggles along the way? Can these experiences help our communal or congregational life as Christians? These were some of the questions that were to be explored.

Contact with another spiritual tradition, however, does not happen in the same way to everyone. Some, dissatisfied with their own tradition, or what they perceived or thought to be their tradition, turn to other traditions in search of a "deeper" or different form of spiritual life. Others discover it almost by accident. Again it is not always the same aspect in the other tradition that attracts all Christians. While meditative practices were for Michael Como the door into the spiritual tradition of Buddhism, Diana Eck in her story says that she was drawn by the Hindu longing to "see" — to have the darsan,' *the vision of God.*

My experience of the spiritual life of a tradition other than my own began when I first went to India in 1965 as a college student. I had been raised and nurtured by a strong social gospel Methodist tradition and had grown up in the mountains of Montana in the American West. I had not come to India seeking spirituality, but rather seeking some understanding of Asia, for my country was engaged in a long and agonizing war in Vietnam.

I lived that year in Banaras and discovered a world of ideas, images, and ways of worship for which nothing in my inherited tradition had prepared me, and to which nothing in my inherited tradition had made any serious response, at least nothing of which I was aware. I say nothing of which I was aware, for I have learned since then a great deal about the dialogue of Hindus and Christians. And yet we live our lives and make our spiritual journeys and crossings with the maps and resources that are available to us at the time.

I was confronted there with religious questions and with images of the divine that challenged my presuppositions, indeed my faith, as a Christian. These were the questions that propelled me into the study of the Hindu tradition, a study which I would describe as a calling, a vocation. Through the years my study has brought me into vibrant relationships of encounter and exchange with Hindu teachers whom I have loved, with Hindu families who have taken me in with hospitality, and with Hindu pilgrims with whom I have travelled and worshipped.

As I reflect on my experience over the years, I would make two affirmations. The first is the spiritual value for me of my struggle with sheer otherness. The Hindu life I encountered at first was not my own, did not resemble my own, and could not be assimilated into my own. The process of coming to understand, however partially, that otherness gave me another perspective from which to discover and understand myself and my own faith. The second is the affirmation of the particular, the manifest, the vivid presence of the divine in all its plurality. Here I must confess I have never been seized as powerfully by the *mahavakya* of the Upanishads as by the shrines and visions of the gods. The ultimate unity of the many paths seemed obvious and easily accessible to me as a Christian. What stretched, challenged, and deepened my religious imagination and spiritual growth more was the overt, playful, manifest and concrete multiplicity of ways of seeing the divine. I cannot say I have appropriated these as "my own", whatever that may mean, but I have come to see through them the meaning of the incarnation.

When I think of God the Incarnate One, who shows himself to us, I see God most clearly in the image of Christ. That is natural, because my eyes and mind have been attuned to see and think with that image since childhood. And yet I recall, some years ago, the incredulous face of an old Hindu man, the cousin of my teacher in Banaras, who asked me one day if it was really true that Christians believe there was but *one* divine incarnation, one *avatara* or divine "descent". Yes, many do, I responded. But how is it possible, he asked, to believe that God showed himself but once, to one people, in one part of the world, and so long ago? The implications were clear in the expression on his face: What kind of God would that be? How stingy such a God would be! What kind of people would believe in such a God? To him it was clear that the full, embodied disclosure of God to men and women was not only multiple in time and place, but potentially infinite, limited only by our capacity to see.

My own capacity to "see" the incarnation has been extended greatly by the faith of Hindus. I have begun to learn to see something of what Hindus see by following along with them in thousands of miles of backroads pilgrimage travel in India to the places where they go to "see" God. They call it *darsan*, literally "seeing" or "beholding" the image of God. One sees and is also seen. One "takes *darsan*" and the divine "gives *darsan*". It is a gift. The image might be famous far and wide, or very ordinary. It might be at the headwaters of a great river, at the top of a hillock, or by the side of the road. The image is a divine embodiment, a divine "descent" as it were. It is not, I learned, something *at* which one looks and, therefore, at which one's vision halts; it is, rather, a lens through which one sees, which focuses and directs one's vision.

The image makes the presence of God available to us, and in serving the image — with food, water, and light, with a fan and a fly-whisk — Hindus practise every day the language of hospitality that the divine presence in this world requires of us.

Let me tell you a specific instance, a day and hour among many, when my encounter with the incarnation was jarred and stretched by the Hindu vision. One morning two years ago I was in Kankroli in rural Rajasthan, in the community of Krishna, where Krishna is honoured as a child. The bells rang for the mid-morning worship and the faithful gathered round the door of Krishna's chamber. I too craned my neck for the first glimpse of the child-god when the doors were opened and the curtain was flung back. Two priests stood before Krishna, but they did not make the usual offerings of lamps, food and water. They proceeded to take out Krishna's toys, his silver tops and miniature cows, and play with them in front of Krishna. I was startled, dumbfounded really, and before long I found myself laughing with delight at the utterly foreign but somehow illumining fact that one might worship the Lord by pleasing him with play.

In Kankroli I confronted the question of incarnation. What does the language of God-with-us, the incarnational language of my own tradition, really mean? Was this offering of play really any different from the many Hindu rites of hospitality and affection — the offering of food, water to wash the feet, a soft bed to rest? And does not all of this familial, ritual language of love and hospitality towards God enable us to practise the presence of the incarnate God in all of life? How better to practise the language of love for the incarnate child, even the child Jesus, than to make an offering of our play?

I will give you another instance of this kind of spiritual encounter, perhaps of the harder and darker side of the incarnation. I lived for several years in the city of Banaras, a city of a thousand temples where life pulses intensely and vibrantly through the streets and lanes. It is also a city of cremation grounds, where death and suffering are visibly and overtly a part of daily life. And yet it is Shiva's holy city, which Hindus speak of as Kashi, the luminous, the divine embodiment of Shiva's radiant light, a *jyotirlinga*. When I first came to Banaras I asked over and over: How could this city, which in some ways is the very epiphany of death, be seen as so holy by Hindus?

I was confronted, again, with the question of the incarnation: How did I expect the Holy to look? Must it really look pure, white, clean, and probably Protestant — the resident, glorious, invisible Christ of the beautiful white, high-steepled churches of New England? Of course not. In Shiva's city I began to see that it is precisely in this place, in the full presence of suffering and death, that Hindus affirm the full and eternal presence of Shiva and the faith of safe-crossing to the far shore. And I realized that if I could not see the point of the faith of Hindus, there in Banaras, I had probably missed the point of my own faith in the incarnate Christ, who abides with us not only in light and life, but in suffering and death. Along the banks of the Ganga and in the lanes of Banaras, life and death have a human face, and it is that same precious humanness that is the subject of the incarnation. Shiva, the supreme light, has a multitude of faces and is present, so they say, at every step.

One final example. There is not one *jyotirlinga*, of course, but many. For Hindus, I found, those things that are truly profound are not marked by singularity and uniqueness. On the contrary, if something is truly significant, it is repeated, duplicated and seen from many angles. One of the other *jyotirlingas* in India is Kedarnath, high in the Himalayas, where the rhythm of worship, morning and night, alternates between the *nirvan arati*, the worship of the unmarked, unclothed, rock of Shiva, and the *srngar arati*, the worship of Shiva decked out with a face of regal splendour. At another in Ujjain in central India, the many faces of Shiva called *jhankis* or "glimpses" are painted in succession on the plain stone shaft. Though the great traditions of the Upanishads, like the mystical traditions of the West, speak of a *via negativa* — *neti, neti, neti*, not this, not this, not this — I have found in my experience that I am not gripped by those insights. Not nearly so profoundly, in any case, as I am gripped by what in India has always been the other side of the coin — *asti, asti, asti*, it is this, it is this, it is this. The unmarked marker of the divine, the *linga*: the many faces and glimpses of the divine. Both are there, and the worship of Shiva weaves them inextricably together. In my experience, however, it is not the ineffable oneness of God that surprises me, delights me, shakes me deeply, and turns me around. It is the astounding multiplicity and particularity of God's incarnate presence.

On the Pilgrim Path

C. MURRAY ROGERS

Those who gathered at Kyoto came from all the major traditions of the church — Orthodox, Roman Catholic and Protestant. But the participants were chosen not because they represented these church traditions or any of the geographical regions. These were persons known to have taken a deep interest in other forms of spirituality; a number of them had practised other spiritual disciplines for 15 to 20 years, and some for an even longer period of time.

Murray Rogers, an Anglican priest from England, for example, has spent nearly 42 years in Asia in what he described as an "open fellowship" with its religious traditions. Over the years, says Rogers, the Holy Spirit helped him "slowly, slowly" to look at the people of other faiths and their spiritual disciplines with "new eyes". He spoke of being "extraordinarily blessed with friends from 'other' spiritual paths" and added: "I have grown to know that there are no 'other faiths' except in the most external and sociological terms." Murray Rogers had experience of ashram life not only in India, but also in Jerusalem, Middle East and Hong Kong. Life for him has been a pilgrimage.

Out of the years, now nearly 42, that I have been fortunate enough to live in Asia, nine were spent in the Old City of Jerusalem. That was long enough to teach me that my earlier accepted belief about "chosen people" was false, untenable in the light of Christ. If, as I firmly believe, "God so loved the world..." (John 3:16), then the idea that some of his children, the Jews and the Christians, were "first class", while others were second or third class, was strictly speaking nonsense, understandable maybe as a mental and psychological trick to lend support to Jewish and Christian self-identity, but incompatible with the mind of Christ. As St Peter discovered to his surprise, "God has no favourites" (Acts 10:34).

That experience in the Holy City of Jews, Christians and Muslims, came after many years in the largely Hindu environment of India, and has been followed by seven years further east once again, on the borders of China, where the Taoist, Confucian and Buddhist winds blow, however imperceptible at times their outward show may be. Extraordinarily blessed with friends from these "other" spiritual paths, I have grown to know that there are no "other faiths" except in the most external and sociological terms. Being allowed myself, by God's grace, to rejoice in and live "by faith", by trust in God as God is made real to me day by day through Christ in the gospel and in the eucharist, I discover as brother, as sister, any person living "by faith", whether a follower of the Sanātana Dharma, of Islam, or of the Buddhist, Jewish or Taoist way. Far from this "thing", faith, being the reality that divides and separates — as it tends to do for the so-called monotheistic families — it is precisely this existential trust in a Reality beyond/within oneself, by whatever name that Reality may be known, that gives us to one another as human beings, belonging, as we do, to each other in this most basic way.

Thanks to what the Spirit has managed slowly, slowly, to teach me over the decades, chiefly through shared faith-experiences with friends of other spiritual paths, the eyes with which I look at them have now a different look; the astigmatic vision that I inherited as a Christian as a result of which I affirm the "finality of Christ" and its concommitant, i.e. that we Christians are the norm, the chosen, the complete, over-against the partial, the "on-the-way", yet to be fulfilled "others", is now, I hope at least, rectified. We are *all* "on the way", we are *all* people of God. I am now convinced (as I have written elsewhere) that "the fundamental message of any of our religions, including my own, lies deeper and beyond the framework in which that message may have been given to the world. The Lord Jesus Christ was not a Christian! True, his message, his work of salvation, was lived out and revealed in a Jewish setting, but it was too strong a message to be confined within that spiritual and cultural packaging."

I think that many of us disciples of Christ, journeying through him to the Father, need that restoration of true vision. That restoration came to me over the years through experiencing even in a very limited way as one of God's special gifts the spiritual and human path of Hindus, of Zen Buddhists, and now most recently of the Taoist sages Chuang Tzu and Lao Tzu. Knowing now, experiencing now, that I am their brother, I am their fellow pilgrim, I gladly share (without fear of disloyalty to Christ and to his band, namely, the church) their treasures of experience, their perceptions of the Mystery, their ways of breathing the Reality beyond all name and form. "I" and "they" have almost disappeared and in their place it is "we". No longer am I driven to fight crusades to bring "them" over to "my" side, as if Christ were on "my" side. Fanaticism, including Christian fanaticism, is seen to be what in fact it always is, an appalling insult to the Divine Mystery lying beyond and within creation.

"The Word was made flesh", and ever since that wonderful event in history the disciples of that Word-made-flesh, as someone has said, led by theologians, have been concerned with turning him back into words! One great gift of my brothers and sisters in Asia, in the families of Hinduism, Buddhism and Taoism, is to convince me that we dare not stop with words or concepts, that the *eidos* level is a false halting-place. Only the "knowledge of God", the vision of God, in the biblical sense of deep experience, counts. I can see now that one can be a brilliant theologian, lecturing, for example, on the Nicene Creed, and "know" nothing of the Divine Mystery, the Holy Trinity, upon whom one is expending a multitude of words. Or, on the other hand, one can be illiterate, unable to write or utter one word about the Reality that fills one, and yet be a deep "practiser" or doer of the Word. To know *about* God, to talk *about* God, to preach *about* prayer, is very different from knowing God, from tasting and practising contemplative prayer. The difference that Hindu friends make between *brahmavādī*, one who talks about Brahman, and *brahmadvid*, one who knows Brahman, has been very largely ignored by us Christians, especially of the Western churches.

The Sanskrit word *sādhana* epitomizes a whole attitude and way of life that has been revealed to me through Hindu and Buddhist friends and this is for me a cause of thankfulness to God. *Sādhana* means spiritual exercise, involving hard work and regular practice; it is your way of living the Reality that has begun to take hold of you, body, mind and spirit. It is the spiritual discipline, way of life, that you take upon yourself because you want the Holy Spirit to transform you into the human being God created you to be. If it is true that it is, as St Paul puts it (Rom. 12:2), God's will for my mind to be remade and my whole nature thus transformed, then my *sādhana* is my practical response in the ordinary life of each day to that divine intention for me.

My *sādhana* will involve a daily timetable in terms of set hours of getting up and going to bed, sensible eating habits, times for silent meditation, worship and prayer, the taking of exercise, the being alert all the time to catch my ego at work before it does further damage to my gradual advance, by God's grace, towards living constantly in consciousness of God. The Bhagavad Gita (12:18-19) puts it like this, and I hear it as the goal of my *sādhana*, my daily spiritual discipline, the longed-for fruit of years of ongoing work, not yet concluded, instigated surely by the Lord himself and dependent upon my response. "Who serves both friend and foe with equal love, not buoyed up by praise or cast down by blame, alike in heat and cold, pleasure and pain, free from selfish attachments and self-will, ever full, in harmony everywhere, firm in faith — such a one is dear to Me," says the Lord. How frequently and how sadly most of us Christians drift, following the mentality and way of life of modern society that again and again encourage in us greed, material and spiritual! The spirit offers to each of us — and in this, I have found, Hindu and Zen friends set us an example — a way to complete integration within my own consciousness of the Lord present and alive as the deepest and most real part of me, my Self (with a capital S).

At the heart of this work of integration lies the steady day-by-day giving of time as a priority for meditation. There is, as some of us have learnt, not only from Christian sources but also and more particularly from Hindu or Buddhist sources, no integration, no descent into the depths of consciousness, into Christ, without the work of silent meditation. True, the deep mystics of our own Christian tradition, St John of the Cross, St Teresa of Avila, Meister Eckhart and a number of others, all taught this way of meditation and life. One can find it in the Philokalia, that spiritual treasure of the Orthodox churches, or one may be directed to it by one of the spiritual guides who have trodden that path themselves. For myself I came to it through the example and teaching of Hinduism and Zen Buddhism which taught me — and still do — the deep meaning of the Lord when he said: "Love the Lord your God with all your heart, with all your soul, with all your mind, and with all your strength — and love your neighbour as yourself" (Mark 12:30-31). There are no short-cuts to such a life in Christ, no "fast food shops" of Christian spirituality.

Much of this flowing together of streams has happened in our experience in what I can only call the eucharistic life which over the decades has gradually become ours. By this expression I do not refer simply to the fact that each day we rejoice to celebrate the eucharist, but that that "happening" has drawn into itself — should I say, Himself? — our own life in Christ and, in a way I find hard to describe, those who follow the Hindu, Buddhist and Taoist paths. They are rarely with us physically at the early hour each day when the eucharist is celebrated, and yet they are, in their scriptures, in their living symbols, whether it be the gong, the incense, the offering of fire *(āratti)*, signs all of them which reach down within our consciousness. Then there are the scriptures and the writings of the eastern sages — the Upanishads or Bhagavad Gita (while we lived in India) to which we have now added the writings of Chuang Tzu and other Chinese sages (living as we do on the borders of China). We read such scriptures daily before we read from the Bible and find that they resonate within each other and are a quite extraordinary strength in our spiritual nutrition. Along with them and at other times in the day, we experience the marvellous riches in Hindu prayers, gathered by us from a multitude of sources and composing what we call our "Hindu prayer book". There are also the songs and hymns of praise from the Vedic scriptures without which we would now be greatly impoverished.

There is of course a proper place for the academic study and scrutiny of scriptures, the work of the intellect, but that always has its limitations. Too often it proceeds no further and is content with mental wrestling to understand mentally the spiritual experience which precedes it. Too often it invalidates itself by being learned thought on what has *not* been experienced, the grappling intellectually with what does not exist for the thinker, if he or she is perhaps a *brahmavādī* only, one who talks about, thinks about, Brahman, the Absolute. It is at this point that so much Christian theology invalidates itself, as becomes painfully obvious to many Hindu and Buddhist practitioners on the way.

The "eastern" paths to spiritual knowledge and awareness have known all along, as indeed the Christian mystics know also, that no man or woman advances far on the path towards the ultimate awakening of the human spirit without a guru or spiritual guide. It is easy to denigrate the guru, a favourite pastime for many Christian people who, in their ignorance of the blessing involved, look scathingly at the pseudo-gurus who flood the spiritual market in the West, but for those, like ourselves, who have begun to taste the experience of being led to a spiritual guide or guru by the Spirit, this is certain to remain one of the deepest gifts of Hinduism, or, in an analogous way, of Zen Buddhism. There are surely very rare exceptions. Ramana Maharshi was one such, whose spirits plumb the depths without the guidance of another human being. But normally the guru is indispensable for anyone who longs to make real progress on the spiritual path. For deep and contemplative prayer most people need a guru, a spiritual guide (to be carefully distinguished from a father confessor or a spiritual director in Western tradition), one to whom he will be led by the Spirit when he is prepared for such a radical encounter, for the guru is the manifestation of God given by God as grace for that final crossing "to the further shore" of the seeker's consciousness, described as *samādhi* or enlightenment but by definition beyond all description. Only when the disciple has already been freed to a very large extent from his/her own ego, from self-concern and self-conceit, when he/she lives beyond the dualities (those mentioned in the earlier quotation from the Bhagavad Gita), will it be safe for the guru who has himself reached the goal to send the disciple through the doorway into that "world" of the Spirit from which there is no return. Having gone through that doorway the disciple (like the master) "attains the fullness of being, the fullness of God himself" (Eph. 3:19). Such a one will normally return to society, to the life of family, work and friends, to his or her experiences and responsibilities as a citizen of the world; within oneself, on the level of deep consciousness, one has "crossed over" for ever to the "other side". Only somebody who has gone further on the human and spiritual path than the present writer can speak of these matters — and such a one will not care to do so!

And this in recapitulation: Swami Abhishiktānanda (Dom Le Saux), the man whom some of us were so blessed to have as friend and teacher, wrote in his personal diary for 15 January 1971 — the personal jottings which were only discovered after his death in December 1973: "Le Christ est trop grand pour être réduit à son expression dans le Nouveau Testament et l'Eglise" ("Christ is too great to be reduced to the expression of him conveyed through the New Testament and the church") He spoke the truth. We Christians are always tempted to fashion Christ according to our own measurements. When, thanks to all that his Hindu and Buddhist brothers and sisters have experienced on their pilgrim path, as well as to his own self-disclosure in "Christian" channels of grace, we discover him as he truly is, always beyond, beyond all name and form, always beyond all his innumerable manifestations, and when we hear his voice sending us beyond ourselves, beyond every experience we may have had of him hitherto, then we know ourselves to be interwoven threads of a tapestry which is beyond our imagining in wonder and glory — and that tapestry is the life of the Father, the Silence in which alone this extraordinary voyage of creation will reach its goal.

May this word of Teilhard de Chardin, a word pointing to adoration, express our gratitude for being allowed a small part in this whole mystery of life:

> Like a vast tide the Being will have dominated the trembling of all beings.
> The extraordinary adventure of the World will have ended in the bosom of a
> tranquil ocean, of which, however, each drop will still be conscious of being
> itself.

Journey Towards an Inclusive Spirituality

M. THOMAS THANGARAJ

Interestingly enough, while Murray Rogers coming out of the Western Christian tradition has learned to accept and adopt the Asian spiritual disciplines with some ease and is able to find the theological language to expound it, Thomas Thangaraj, an Indian Christian, testifies to a different relationship to his Hindu environment. His story raises a number of questions of identity and relationship. Thangaraj's story is likely to echo the life of many Christians in Asia.

I come from a small village called Nazareth in south Tamil Nadu, India. Nearly two hundred years ago, the people in my village embraced Christianity and changed the name of the village from "Chanpattu" to "Nazareth". A church with a tall steeple was built in the centre of the village and the village was reorganized with the church as focal point. I lived in similar villages all through my childhood. Therefore I operated with what might be called a ghetto-spirituality. The only reality I knew was the Christian church, with its choir, school, and other programmes. I had practically no exposure to people of other faiths. Though I had a few classmates in school who were Hindus and Muslims, we never talked about each other's religions. But at the same time, my spirituality was celebrative and communitarian. I was impelled always to help the poor among my friends. I used to keep a small bottle which contained paper ashes mixed with coconut oil to apply as first aid to anyone who was injured.

As a boy of seven I once visited a famous Hindu temple in a nearby village while its annual festival was going on. Animal sacrifice was offered in the temple and I witnessed it with a certain curiosity mixed with fear. The strange noises, the smell of goats and blood, and the splashing colours in the vicinity evoked in me a sense of awe. I could not really make much of this event, though it had forcefully impressed on me the strangeness and depth of my Hindu neighbour's spirituality.

As a college student I came to have a lot of doubts and questions about the Christian heritage. There was a streak of rebellion in me, and I tended to reject the Christian tradition as non-sensical. But towards the end of my undergraduate course I went through a powerful experience of conversion in evangelical and fundamentalist terms. A new spiritual vigour took hold of me and I dedicated myself to the ministry of the church. All traditional spiritual exercises such as Bible-reading, personal and family and prayer worship now began to make sense. I was actively involved in verbal proclamation of the good news of Jesus Christ to others, especially "non-Christians". The Christian faith was crystal clear to me and therefore I found myself compelled to engage myself in witnessing by word. The spirituality of this period in my life can be called "exclusive spirituality". It was very clear to me at that time that nothing "Hindu" could have any place in my life or spirituality.

With this exclusive spirituality I moved to Serampore in West Bengal to do my first theological studies as preparation for the ordained ministry of the church. Theological education put a definite question-mark on my earlier understanding and practice of spirituality. I was led to look for alternate forms of spirituality. More than all the lectures, reading, and studying, my lively contact with Hindus in Serampore challenged me to move towards an inclusive spirituality. My interest in music led me to unexpected situations of direct encounter with Hindu spirituality. My Hindu friends used to invite me to their festivals, especially Durga Puja, to perform music during the festivities. There I was, standing in front of the image of Durga and playing "non-Christian" music. This was really a spiritual crisis. But these Hindus were my *friends* and I dared not say "no" to their invitation. Yet my spirituality had now to accommodate this "spiritual" experience. Thus the first step was taken towards an inclusive spirituality.

At this point, I should say a word about the place of music in my life. After my conversion I had decided not to play anything other than Christian songs and music. This was how I stumbled into composing and setting to music my own songs. I was a member of the orchestra of Heber Hall at the Madras Christian College while I studied there. I had to play film songs. I was so disturbed by this that I approached the conductor of the orchestra and asked him whether I could leave the orchestra because I did not believe in playing film songs. He took me aside and gently told me: "Thomas, music is a divine thing; please do not lock it up within narrow religious boundaries." At that time my spirituality could not open my music to wider horizons.

After my ordination I was assigned a town parish with seven other village parishes. I was expected to pastor all the eight congregations. This meant that I would have to celebrate the eucharist at least five times every Sunday. This involved an element of drudgery which had its impact on my spirituality. The tendency to sink into a kind of "mechanical spirituality" was very real. But the simple, celebrative, and lively spirituality of my village congregations kept my spiritual life alive. I did a few experiments with indigenous music in the worship and it was a rewarding experience. The most challenging experience during this period came when I was asked to teach "moral education" to a group of Hindu and Muslim students in a local Christian college. During the first meeting, I asked the students what they would like to study and discuss in the moral education course. They all said with one voice: "Why don't you teach us Christianity?" I was at first shocked and then challenged by their openness to other faiths. At the end of the course, I found that my spirituality was very enriched and strengthened by the openness of the Hindu and Muslim students.

Then as a theological teacher I have been enabled to open myself to more and more incorporation of Hindu spirituality and spiritual exercises into worship and daily Christian life. The use of Hindu bhajans, especially from the Tamil Saivite tradition, has become a part of my spiritual journey. I have also been exposed to the question of integrating two kinds of spiritualities, spirituality of contemplation and spirituality of combat. My own involvement in inter-religious dialogue with my Hindu friends and my colleagues' involvement in the socio-political reality of Indian society have forced me to look to an integration of these two experiences.

Let me mention two experiences to illustrate this. I am a member of the Saivite-Christian study group which meets regularly to engage in inter-religious dialogue. On Good Friday last year we met to discuss the question of suffering in the light of the cross. We were there, Saivites and Christians, together at the foot of the cross. The Saivite friends shared their spirituality with us and helped us to have a fresh "spiritual" experience of the cross. How much more real and radiating the cross of Christ was that evening! How much deeper our experience of the cross was in the company of Saivites! There was a conversation going on in the depths of our being. It was a dialogue between the hearts and "spirits" of our group, hovered over by the the the Spirit of the loving and living God!

Recently I visited a small village near Madurai where a group of harijans (low caste people) were assaulted by the upper caste people in the village. We met the people and talked to them about the incident. The harijans were depressed and in despair. We consoled them and discussed how they might claim the justice that is due to them. Our conversation with them was a spiritual experience in which we felt once again the reality of the cross. There was no mention of "God" in that conversation but we felt the presence of the hovering Spirit of God which creates cosmos out of chaos.

I can go on narrating incidents of this kind which help us to see the need for an integration of contemplative spirituality with the spirituality for combat. It is clear that a spirituality for our times demands such a creative integration.

My whole journey has been one of opening up my spirituality to be inclusive, step by step, and more and more. It has come to be inclusive of Hindu openness, Hindu musical traditions and the spiritual exercises of other faiths. But the question can be asked: How inclusive can we be? How far can we go in our journey? The creative Spirit of God, I believe, will lead me into unknown and unforeseen paths of inclusiveness.

In Search of Being one with the One

MATAJI VANDANA

There were others, however, who did not feel their identity threatened by the Hindu environment. They were open to adopting Hindu spiritual disciplines; they made a distinction between spirituality and "practices" and "disciplines" that help one in one's spiritual life. Spirituality, it was remarked, is life in or guided by the Spirit. Spiritual disciplines are practices that sustain and enhance this life. Mataji Vandana says that Christian spirituality is life lived in the spirit of Christ. But in so doing she has over many years adopted from the spiritual traditions of Hinduism practices "that are in keeping with the spirit of Christ". What does this mean? We asked Mataji to tell us what practices were adopted in her ashram, and she showed how the three ways (margas) *to God — the way of devotion, the way of knowledge, and the way of action — have been integrated into one in the context of ashram life. Jeevan Dhara (the Living Streams) in the Himalayas, established by Mataji, is a place where both Christians and Hindus share ashram life. Christian life and practice here are shaped by the spiritual disciplines of the threefold yoga.*

By "spirituality" I understand life lived according to the Spirit. A "spiritual person" is one who lives in and is guided by the Spirit. Christian spirituality is lived by one who has the Spirit of Christ. A Christian then can adopt any practices of other faiths that are in keeping with the Spirit of Christ. One need eschew only what is contrary to the spirit of the gospel. "He that is not against me is with me," said Jesus. In the light of this, how have the practices I have adopted from Hinduism/Buddhism helped me to live my Christian spirituality?

First of all I should like to say that I have adopted more than just some practices. I have accepted a way of life; a life-style from the age-old yogic tradition of India, which I find very evangelical. What is it to practise yoga? Is it different from living according to the gospel? Dr Ramsay, Archbishop of Canterbury, once asked Swami Venkateshanand, a Hindu guru of repute and of great breadth of vision: "If my religion, my faith, my practices, my approach to God, all this leads me there, would you still want me to practise yoga?" The Swami answered: "You *are* a yogi, you are using different terminology and that's not important."[1]

My "practices" of the various yogas, then, are set within the yogic life-style which can be lived anywhere. Mine happens to be lived in an ashram — another indigenous tradition which helps one live an Indian Christian spirituality more naturally in a yogic atmosphere.[2]

A yogic way of life helps "harmonize" or "unite" not only me to myself (my body, psyche and spirit "oned") and me to my outer environment or to God, but also one that harmonizes my practice of Christian spirituality with that of my own country's culture and religious practices. Though "yoga" comes from the Hindu tradition, practised for centuries before it was systematized by Patanjali, it is a-religious and can therefore be practised by people of any faith or no faith. It is evident that I am not speaking here of yoga in the popular, constricted sense of Hatha yoga (body postures or *asanas*) as the word is often used or misused. Though yoga is a goal — in the sense that it means "union". Yoga also means a "way", even as — and I say this respectfully — Our Lord Jesus is "the way" to life and union with the Father. Since it is a way of life, it might be appropriate to run through our day in the ashram — showing how the various yogic *margas* (ways) are practised by us.

Our day begins with *pratah sandhya*[3] (early morning prayer/worship) — preceded by *asana, prananayama*, meditation, and followed by the liturgy and paraliturgy. At mid-day we have *madhyan sandhya* for peace of the world after some *japa yoga*; and again in the evening, *sayyam sandhya*, preceded by an hour's community meditation.

All these community *sandhyas* involve our using *jnana, hatha, bhakti, japa* and *raja* yoga as we shall see presently. In between these focal points of the day we perform various duties and work in the spirit of *karma* yoga.

Jnana yoga (wisdom, using our intellect): The scripture readings for the liturgy as for the *sandhyas*, always include relevant passages from other scriptures, mostly from the *Upanishads* and the Bhagavad Gita. They all lead to the wisdom that is Truth, and helps us "enter into the radiance of the Supreme Spirit who is greater than all greatness" (*Mundaka Up*.2.8). Reading other scriptures often throws light on our own;

they illumine texts with which one has long been familiar, yet which one has not yet really begun to fathom. Swami Abhishiktananda was the first to initiate me into reading the Bible in the light of other scriptures. This had led me to exciting new pastures for my own theologizing and spiritual life, and hopefully for some others.[4]

The study of and reflection and meditation on the word according to this yoga of wisdom, leading one to know the Self, is done in three steps — the first two very similar to St Ignatius' first method of meditation.

a) *Shravanam* — listening to (or reading) the word; listening with the heart — as Mary must have heard the word God spoke to her through the angel Gabriel. "Let the scriptures be thy authority as to what is right and what is not right. Know the words of the scriptures and do in this life the work to be done" (Bhagavad Gita 16.24). "If you love me you will keep my word" (John 14:15).

b) *Mananam* — is reflecting on the word in the light of one's own life and needs. This leads to the final and most important step. Often unremembered and unpractised in the Christian's way of meditating on the scriptures — viz:

c) *Nididhyasanam* — when the truth reflected upon is taken down from the mind (which possessed the truth) to the heart (which is possessed by it) in silence. As St John of the Cross says, the One Word which proceeded from the Silence that is the Father leads us back to that Silence. Only in silence can that Word be heard which transforms us into Itself. "In truth who knows God, becomes God" (*Mundaka Up* 2.9). The word thus held in loving silence alone can divinize us — the *theosis* of which the Eastern Christians were not shy to speak. This holding the word in silence gradually delivers us from the unreal leading us to the Real (*Brihadaranyaka Up* 1.3.28), from "the great illusion" which sees the One as two; and "when one sees God (everywhere) one is free from all fetters" (*Svetasvatara Up.* 1.5 and 12).

The "seeds of the Word," as Vatican II calls non-biblical scriptures, have indeed much to teach us, and the way some of our forward-looking theologians are thinking today, a day might come when we may no more speak of them as "seeds" but as "the word of God". For God did speak only one word — in sundry times and myriad ways. Perhaps we have not yet ears to hear. But living in a religiously pluralistic country like India, one's *theologizing* cannot but be constantly challenged. If one is rooted in Christ, it can be an exciting exploration, an opening into wide horizons, a climbing into deeper depths in "the cave of the heart".

Of course this involves risks, but some who have had the courage to take them have climbed Calvary like the Master, but have also, like him, seen the glory and crossed (passed over) "the bridge supreme that leads to immortality" (*Svet. Up.* 6.19).[5]

Bhakti Yoga — the way of loving devotion — followed by the vast majority of Hindus, as indeed of all people, naturally needs to permeate all our devotions — at the liturgical worships and *sandhyas*, as well as our personal prayer life. The Sanskrit chants are taken from the Hindu scriptures, the songs of devotion *(bhajans)* from the *Bhaktas*, the great Hindu poet-saints. We sing mostly the compositions of Kabir, Tulsi, Surdas, Meera, etc., in North India, or of Tukaram, Namdev, Eknath, the Christian poet Narayan Vaman Tilak of Maharashtra. They set us aflame with the same fire as do our Christian mystics for whom "Jesu" was "fire, song, honey" (cf. Richard Rolle). If *The Cloud of Unknowing* tells us: "By love may he be caught and held, by thinking never," the Bhagavad Gita says: "Only by love can men see me and know and come unto me" (11.5.4.). Often the words are utterly Christian in their theology; at other times they are Christian in spirit. However, wisdom and discretion require a certain sensitivity in the selection of these songs (as of scripture passages) of other traditions — depending on who are the participants at worship.

Sharing Hindu *feasts* and adapting them to our needs is yet another way of sharing our faith and love in our dialogue, e.g., we integrate into our liturgy the celebration of *Deepavali*, the festival of lights; *Raksha-Bandhan* festivals celebrating various *seasons*; national days like Gandhi's birthday, etc. All these increase *bhakti* towards God and fellowship with people of other faiths.

Arati is the Hindu rite of waving a light before an image or a person worthy of honour. It is a form of praise and veneration. We do it at every liturgy and *sandhya*; only we wave the light first to the Lord present in the blessed sacrament, to the word (the Bible), to the images of the Blessed Virgin and the saints, then — and this is our own creation — to those present in whom too is the Real Presence; and finally to those living out in the village and to the Lord of the mountains visible outside (the Himalayas) recalling the verse in the Gita: "Among mountains I am the Himalayas" (10.25).

At the end we recall how the Lord Jesus, "the light of the world", also called us that; and therefore when taking the flame to our eyes and into us, we pledge ourselves anew, as it were, to try and be that light to others. While the light of the camphor (a symbol of total offering, of our utterly consuming ourselves; leaving, like the camphor, no ashes of the ego-self) is still burning, we pray for the dying whose lives are flickering at that moment between life and death, that they may have courage and confidence. When the flame dies out before us, we recite the "requiems" — for the repose of the souls who have just left their bodies.

Guru-pad-puja is yet another meaningful adaptation of a Hindu ritual observed in many ashrams on Thursdays (called *guruvar*, the day of the gurus), when *guru-bhakti* — loving devotion for the Master — is dramatically expressed. We observe it too in our ashram: only, instead of washing the feet of the human guru or the *acharya* (teacher) or the head of the ashram, the latter washes the feet of all present and anoints them — after we have read John 13:1-17 showing how Jesus turns the world's values upside down. In the light of this often touching ceremony, we reflect on our attitude to work to see if it is truly "service".

Karma yoga — selfless service. Work, which fills the greater part of our day, is meant to become in reality a "yoga" — our work as a "means" of uniting us to God — not an obstacle dichotomizing work and contemplation as is our wont. The weekly Guru-pad-puja, as seen above, reminds and challenges us to examine our attitudes to work: whether it is truly service rendered unselfishly, without seeking any reward or expectation or whether we look on work "with the genesis attitude" — as a punishment and a necessary evil, rather than using our human gifts and talents to express God's power in us — our "innermost self" in a creative way for the welfare of others.

It teaches us, too, to distinguish not only between work and *seva* (service) but also between agitation and activity; to know that contemplation is truly the highest of all human activities; that the test of our work being truly a "yoga" and a "oneing" is whether we do all works, no matter what, high or low, with equal attention and enthusiasm, not regarding the person for whom we do it, but seeing only the Lord. No wonder Hindu spiritual practice pays so much stress on continually being engaged in *karma yoga*; it is a primary purifying prerequisite of all other *sadhanas* (spiritual efforts or practices).

Japa yoga, the oldest of all yogas, supposedly going back 5,000 years, enables one to "pray without ceasing" all through one's day and even in sleep — once the "prayer" (mantra) has taken root. "Japa" commonly translated as "repetition" is shown by Patanjali to be much more: "a constant awareness of what is signified by *Om*" viz., God (*Yoga Sutras* 1.28). Christians no doubt are familiar with the "Prayer of Jesus" of the Orthodox Church, but certain specific practices of this yoga known to

Hindus have been found of great help by individuals, e.g. *likhit japa* (writing the name beautifully and concentratedly as part of one's daily *sadhana*), long-protracted practices for many days and weeks of repeating the Name while keeping strict silence and fast, etc.[6] We sing the japa together as community at midday *sandhya* to calm ourselves down before praying for peace of the world. Personally, I have found this yoga a help to inner awareness.

Hatha yoga, the most recent of all yogic practices (since the twelfth century A.D.) and yet the most popular and often misunderstood today both in the East and the West, also forms part of our daily spiritual practices. The *asanas* (bodily postures) and the *pranayama* (breath regulation or control) are not for us just for physical fitness, but a preparatory means for remaining steady and concentrated for meditation, as well as being used as a beautiful form of prayer. "With my body I thee worship."

Thus the *surya namaskar* (salutation to the sun) is done with certain mantras for each of the twelve movements.[7] We have also put them to psalm-verses to suit each posture, partly to act as a pedagogical aid to the Christian, if yet a novice at this yoga. Thus:
— Stand quietly before Yahwe; wait patiently for his coming (Ps. 37:7).
— My God I love you from the depths of my being (Ps. 40:8).
— Come Yahwe, light up my darkness (Ps. 18:28), etc.
But apart from the actual "exercises" making the body fit, flexible and pure, how the practice of *asanas* can help our spiritual life is again brought home to us by Patanjali. He defines *asanas* as a bodily posture which is steady and comfortable, which comes about through total relaxation of effort (which may surprise some who bring even to prayer an achievement-oriented, competitive spirit), and through a state of mind in harmony with the infinite state of repose (*anantam*) (47-48). Thus when holding the opposition physically, the mind is fixed on the *anantam* within. Establishment in *asana* brings about a state in which one is unaffected by the *dvandvas* (the pairs of opposites — heat/cold, pleasure/pain, etc.) (48). One becomes free of external pressures/circumstances, as well as of internal enslavements, thus enabling one's spirit to respond better to the calls of the Holy Spirit within. One begins little by little to experience in one's flesh the profound meaning of "this is my body" and that I am "the temple of the Holy Spirit" — quite a far cry from knowing it only cerebrally from my theology!

The benefits of *asanas* are not confined to the body alone. The psyche and the spirit are also naturally affected — and through the whole day.

Doing the simple *tadasana* (the mountain posture) one begins to realize — experientially — what it means to be so "rooted in the soil of his steadfast love" that one will not be easily shaken by externals, one learns to become and remain steady like the mountain when the stormy winds blow. Doing the *asanas* well, slowly, prayerfully, teaches me to move graciously, doing only one movement/action at a time. This helps one during the day to practise the Buddhist wisdom of *mindfulness* — "keeping my consciousness fully in the present moment", in the here and now.

Pranayama — the second component of hatha yoga — teaches precisely this. Regulation of breath (as also breath awareness) calms the disturbed mind, soothes the seething spirit, restores equilibrium and composure. If *asanas* prepare the body to be still during meditation, *pranayama* prepares the mind to be less like a "drunken monkey" and to become *one-pointed*. It leads one to the next "limb" of yoga –- viz., *pratyahara* — learning to withdraw one's senses from external objects which tend to lure us away from our inmost and real self instead of constantly "returning within". To acquire silence of heart is indeed a long, serious and steady science. As Seraphim of Sarov said: "Acquire inward silence and thousands around you will find salvation." For this reason we keep Fridays as our day of silence from the Hindu practice of *mauna*, the silence of one whose mind is fixed on the One. Fasting helps the "silence" of the body — it makes the silence of the mind a greater reality.

Gradually I began to develop my power of concentration *(dharana)* and hopefully now I do a little meditation *(dhyana)*, waiting with the saints on earth for that delectable goal of "meditation" as Swami Sivananda defines it — "an unceasing flow of God consciousness" — the flow of that Living Water *(Jeeevan Dhara)* promised by Christ, the Great Yogi, to "anyone" who thirsts; "and out of his heart shall flow streams of living water". John tells us: "This he said of the Holy Spirit" (John 7:37-39).

There is very much indeed that I owe to "practices from other faiths" which have led me gradually to learn continually that he who is in the sun fire is the same as the One in the heart of man; "and he who knows this is one with the One".

NOTES

[1] Swami Venkatesananba and Fr Terence Melvin OSM, *Christ, Krishna and You*, Chiltern Yoga Foundation, 1983, p.23.

[2] An "ashram", according to the Hindu tradition, is a place of meeting between a master and a disciple and the life they live together. I had the good fortune to spend several years in Hindu ashrams in Rishikesh, and found a man of God as my guru. The riches I learned there for my Christian life I have described elsewhere. (Vandana, *Gurus, Ashrams and Christians,* London, Darton, Longman Todd, 1978). There are many Christian religious communities or houses of prayer in India today which call themselves "ashrams," but not all fulfill the conditions of such a life.

[3] *Sandhya* — at dawn and dusk (when day and night embrace) and at mid-day (when the sun is at its zenith), replace the church's hours of office (lauds, none, vespers).

[4] Cf. Vandana, *Waters of Fire,* Madras, CLS, 1980 — out of print! St John's Gospel in the light of Vedanta.

[5] Cf. Swami Abhishiktananda, *Montée au fond du coeur* — his *Intimate Journal,* Paris, Oieul, 1986.

[6] Cf. Vandana, *Nama-Japa* — Prayer of the Name in the Hindu and Christian Traditions. Bharatiya Vidya Bhavan, Bombay.

[7] Beautiful invocations are said, like: "Salutations to you who are the friend of all" (meaning "Make us reverence all creatures without discrimination — like the sun"); *Salutations* to the Shining One; to the One who dispels the darkness of our delusions; to the One who nourishes us with energy, etc.

Interiority, Awareness and Realization

SWAMI AMALDAS

A similar story of intense spiritual search and copious adaptation was recounted by Swami Amaldas, a Christian from Kerala, India. His search led him for years to live as a mendicant, begging for his food and spending most of the time in meditation in the forest. Eventually he became part of the ashram community at Shantivanam started by two French fathers, Jules Monchanin, who assumed the name Parama Arubi Ananda (meaning the Bliss of the Supreme Spirit) and Henri Le Saux, well-known as Swami Abhishiktananda (the Bliss of Christ). Today Swami Amaldas lives in a Hindu-Christian dialogue community called Saccidananda ashram in Madhya Pradesh in Central India. The ashram had adopted a number of Hindu practices both for its life-style and for worship.

The Second Vatican Council, in its Declaration on the Relationship of the Church to Non-Christian Religions, said that the church rejects nothing that is true and holy in these religions, and encouraged Catholics to recognize, preserve and promote the spiritual and moral values as well as the social and cultural values to be found among them. Following this direction the All-India Seminar in 1969, which was attended by the whole hierarchy and many representatives of the Catholic Church in India, spoke of the wealth of truth, goodness and beauty in India's religious tradition as "God's gifts to our nation from ancient times". The seminar showed the need for a liturgy closely related to the Indian cultural tradition, and a theology "lived and pondered in the vital context of the Indian spiritual tradition". In particular the need was expressed to establish authentic forms of monastic life in keeping with the best traditions of the church and of the spiritual heritage of India.

Among the gifts given by God to India, the greatest is that of interiority, the awareness of the presence of God dwelling in the heart of every human person, which is fostered by prayer and meditation, by contemplative silence and the practice of yoga and sannyasa.

The aim of our ashram, therefore, following the directions of the All-India Seminar, is to bring into our Christian life the riches of Indian spirituality, to share in that profound experience of God which originated in the Vedas, was developed in the Upanishads and the Bhagavad Gita, and has come down to us today through a succession of sages, yogis and holy men and women. From this experience of God, lived in the context of an authentic Christian life, it is hoped that we may be able to assist the growth of a genuine Indian Christian liturgy, theology and spirituality.

Saccidananda ashram, Shantivanam, the ashram of the Holy Trinity, was founded in 1950 by two French fathers. By taking Indian names and giving the ashram the name Saccidananda (Being-Consciousness-Bliss) a Hindu term for the Godhead here used as a symbol of the three persons of the Christian Trinity, they intended — anticipating the Second Vatican Council and the All-India Seminar — to show that they sought to identify themselves with the Hindu search for God, the quest of the Absolute, which has inspired monastic life in India from the earliest times. They also intended to relate this quest to their own experience of God in Christ in the mystery of the Holy Trinity. Unfortunately Father Monchanin died in 1957 before the ashram could be properly established, and Swami Abhishiktananda, after a few years, settled as a hermit in the Himalayas, where he died in 1973.

Upon Swami Abhishiktananda's departure in 1968, the ashram was taken over by a group of monks under the leadership of Father Bede Griffiths from Kurisumala Ashram in Kerala. Since 1980, Saccidananda ashram, Shantivanam, has been part of the Benedictine order.

Father Bede Griffiths, a Benedictine monk from England, came to India in 1955. He was brought up in the European Benedictine tradition and all that he wanted at first was to establish a monastery in India exactly on the same lines as in England. That would have meant following the Christian way within the Greco-Roman ethos and culture. In fact with an Indian monk he established a monastery of this kind in Bangalore. But within a year or two he discovered his mistake and closed down the monastery. His growing acquaintance with Hindus and Hindu religion, Indian culture and the life-style and simplicity of Indian villages opened his eyes to a new vision of Christian monastic life in India. Soon he came to the conviction that Christian monastic spirituality and way of life must be integrated with Hindu monastic spirituality and way of life, Christian religion must become incarnate in the Indian soil, and he himself must go through a rebirth.

In 1958 Father Bede Griffiths joined Father Frances Acharya who came to India from a Cistercian monastery in Belgium. Together they founded a contemplative monastery, Kurisumala ashram, in Kerala in the diocese of the Syro-Malankara Church. They began to adopt the customs of a Hindu ashram such as the saffron-coloured habit of the Indian sannyasi, sitting on the floor for prayer and meals and so on. Kurisumala ashram has grown over the years as a well established community. I joined this community in 1967. I was from a traditional Syrian Catholic family in Kerala.

In 1971 I rejoined Father Bede Griffiths at Saccidananda ashram, Shantivanam. In 1986 we opened a new ashram in a predominantly Hindu area in the central part of India. The Catholic Bishop of Jabalpur had offered us some land. Until recently it was in the charge of a Norbertine father, who has now retired and wants to end his days as a hermit at Benares on the Ganges. I have been assigned to lay the groundwork and I hope to develop it as a centre for meditation, yoga and inter-religious dialogue in the context of the poor and simple life of the Hindus who are our neighbours. This ashram also is called Saccidananda.

We begin our community prayers with the "Gayatri Mantra" which every devout Brahmin would chant three times a day.

> Salutation to the word which is present on the earth, the heavens, and that which is beyond. Let us meditate on the glorious splendour of that divine Giver of life. May he illuminate our meditation.

For evening prayer we sing a hymn on Saccidananda, the Triune God, in Sanskrit, which was composed by Swami Brahma Bandhab Upadhyaya, one of the first Christian sannyasis in India. At our prayer we have chanting and readings from the Vedas, the Upanishads and the Bhagavad Gita as well as from Tamil and Hindi devotional literature, and psalms and other passages from the Bible, and we make use of Sanskrit and other Indian languages for bhajans (songs), accompanied by drums and cymbals.

In our prayer we make use of various symbols drawn from Hindu traditions, in order to adapt our Christian prayer and worship to Indian traditions and customs. In the morning prayer we use sandalwood. Sandalwood is considered to be the most precious wood and is therefore seen as a symbol of divinity. As it has a sweet fragrance, it is also seen as a symbol of divine grace. We place it on the head and the hands as a way of consecrating the body and its members to God.

At the midday prayer we use the purple powder known as *kumkumum*. This is placed on the spot between the eyebrows and is a symbol of the "third eye". The third eye is the eye of wisdom; whereas the two eyes are the eyes of duality, which see the outer world and the outer self, the third eye is the inner eye which sees the inner light. According to the gospel, if your eye is single, the whole body will be full of light. This single eye is the third eye which was often marked on Greek icons of Christ and is thus a universal symbol. In India red is considered to be the feminine colour, the mark of the mother goddess. We consider that it symbolizes feminine wisdom and apply it to our Lady of wisdom. It should be observed that the midday prayer is a wisdom prayer, consisting of the wisdom psalm (118) and a reading from one of the books.

At the evening prayer we use ashes *(vibhuti)*. The symbolism here is not merely that of Ash Wednesday. Ash is matter from which the impurities have been burnt away. It is the symbol of the human body. This body has to be offered as a sacrifice to God as Jesus offered himself as a sacrifice to God. Placing the ashes on the forehead signifies that our sins and impurities have been burnt away. It is a sign of transformation.

By using these symbols representing the body, mind and soul, we are able to pray with our whole being. At the end of each prayer we offer *arati* before the blessed sacrament. Arati consists in the waving of lights or incense as a sign of honour or worship. It may be done before any sacred thing or person. The root meaning of arati before the central shrine in a temple seems to be this. The inner sanctuary of a temple is always kept dark to signify that God dwells in the darkness in the cave of the heart. When light is waved before the shrine it reveals, as it were, the hidden God. We have lights before the blessed sacrament to manifest the hidden Christ and we then take the light of Christ to our eyes by placing the hands over the flame which is passed round to the congregation.

At the offertory of the mass we make a fourfold offering of the four elements, water, earth, air and fire. Every Hindu puja consists in this offering of the elements to God as a sign of the offering of the whole creation. We first sprinkle water round the altar to purify the altar. Then we sprinkle water on the people to purify the people. The priest then takes a sip of water to purify his inward being. We then offer the fruits of the earth, the bread and the wine, and then eight flowers which are placed around the tali on which the gifts are offered. The eight flowers which are offered with Sanskrit chants represent the eight directions of space and signify that the mass is offered in the centre of the universe thus relating it to the whole creation. We then do arati with incense representing the air and then with camphor representing the fire. Thus the mass is seen to be a cosmic sacrifice in which the whole creation together with all humanity is offered through Christ to the Father.

The ashram seeks to be a place of meeting for Hindus and Christians and people of all religions or none who are genuinely seeking God. We have a guest house where both men and women can stay for retreat and recollection and for religious dialogue and discussion. There is a good library which contains not only books on the Bible and Christian philosophy and theology, but also a representative selection of books on Hinduism and Buddhism and other religions. We have many visitors who come to us from many parts of India and from all over the world; they are seeking God by way of different religious traditions. The ashram serves as a spiritual centre where people can pursue study and meditation.

The ashram is also concerned to help the people in the neighbouring villages. There is a nursery school in one village, where forty to fifty children are cared for every day. Two spinning units have been set up in another village, where sixty girls are employed. The ashram supports itself partly by cultivating the land and partly through contributions from well-wishers. But the central emphasis is to help people grow in the knowledge of God. The ashram is a place where Christian yoga spirituality can be developed. The term yoga comes from the Sanskrit "yug", which means to join or yoke together. So yoga means union; it is the union within oneself, union between the male and the female in oneself, union between the divine and human in oneself. It is the union of the physical, psychic or mental and spiritual in oneself. Yoga means union between human beings, and between human beings and the rest of creation. Above all yoga means the union of human beings with God. In order to grow in the yoga of harmony — the yogic consciousness — the ancient Indian yoga system provides a systematic method which is physically, psychologically and spiritually well balanced and integrated.

A Journey
with the Unknown

BETTINA BÄUMER

*Some of the participants rejected the ideas of "accepting", "adopting",
"using", etc. of other spiritual disciplines and techniques. They looked at
their journey as "going beyond" the limitations of particular traditions in
order to participate in the Spirit which is beyond all names and forms.
The problem about "adopting" other practices, says Bettina Bäumer, is
that it presupposes that these practices can be isolated; spiritual life in
her view is a "totality". "If one allows it to unfold with all its implications
one may be surprised at the transformation taking place."*

Dialogue at the spiritual level is certainly not sufficient if spirituality is
only talked about. But the moment one gets involved in living spirituality
in the meeting with another religious tradition, one discovers that
spiritualities are not closed vessels. They may be different ways of letting
the Spirit take possession of one's life, but we cannot talk of the Spirit in
the plural. If spiritualities, of whatever denomination, are authentic, they
cannot but be living means of communication since what they communicate in is the Spirit.

This, however, does not imply a chaotic confusion of ways and
traditions, for it is valid only at the deepest level. As a stone thrown into
still water creates circular waves on the surface, any deep spiritual
experience has its repercussions increasingly at the external levels of
religion. Even within one tradition, for instance the Christian one, a stone
thrown into the depth can create an explosion on the surface, as is evident
from the lives of most mystics and saints, much more so when this
happens in and through contact with another faith. Swami Abhishiktananda, who had lived such an experience in two traditions with the
utmost sincerity and depth, spoke about such "explosions" towards the

end of his life. Maybe the outer rings of the waves created by his experience are yet to appear and become effective in the church. It is much more comfortable for any institution, the churches not excluded, to look at such an experience from a safe distance and go on with business as usual, than to take it seriously and accept the consequences.

If I am to say something about my own experience, after living in close contact with Indian — mainly Hindu — spirituality for 24 years, I only want to stress a few points which seem important to me.

My attitude at the beginning, and the attitude of my teachers and predecessors on this path, i.e. Christians wanting to incorporate some of the spiritual values of Hinduism or Buddhism in their own way, was certainly one of openness, wanting to learn and being ready to receive inspiration from Indian spirituality for my own inner life as a Christian. But I was not conscious of the full implications of entering into another spiritual world. I felt fairly firm in my Christian faith and wanted to deepen and enrich my spiritual life in India (by "India" I do not mean the geographical reality, but a living spiritual tradition, predominantly "Hindu"). I can still feel this attitude in many of my good Christian friends. We could compare it to somebody wanting to bathe in a river without getting wet!

First of all the question may be asked, why was I attracted towards Hindu spirituality to such an extent that I wanted to immerse myself in this spiritual dialogue? One may find many reasons — psychological, sociological, theological — but the main reason seems to me that I was not satisfied with the way Christian spirituality is lived today. I had discovered the mystical dimension of Christianity, but I could not help feeling that this dimension was suffocated by and suppressed under heavy institutional (legal) and theological (mental) structures. In Hindu spirituality I found that breath of freedom which is so necessary for the full inner growth of the spirit.

What I came to realize was that "adopting practices from other faiths" was not completely honest towards "other faiths" — as if one had the right to extract certain beautiful experiences, practices or teachings from another tradition in order merely to incorporate them in one's own. No wonder that this attitude of "appropriation" or "utilization" practised by Christians has now led to the suspicion on the part of Hindus and Buddhists that this is a kind of spiritual theft. After all, Christians would also feel apprehensive if some Hindus started celebrating the mass without understanding the totality of meaning of which the mass is a part. If we take another tradition seriously, we must also accept its premises —

in the case of the Hindu tradition one such premise is what is called *guruparampara,* the living transmission from master to disciple which alone bestows the *adhikara,* the right to do certain spiritual practices, as well as the power and promise that they will be fruitful.

Another reason why the "adoption of practices from other faiths" is not satisfactory is that it seems to presuppose that these practices can be isolated, whereas spiritual life is a totality. I could have easily said that what I learnt from Hinduism was a way of meditation — but in fact this meditation leads to a transformation of life itself, of one's experience of oneself, of others, of nature, of God. Meditation is not a particular yoga technique, or a zen way of "sitting", taken out of their context. If one allows it to unfold with all its implications, one may be surprised at the transformation that is taking place.

Once I accept all the implications, the next question will be justified: how can one belong to two spiritual traditions at the same time? Does it not lead to either schizophrenia or dishonesty? It is precisely here where I am completely naked and exposed and depend on nothing but divine grace. There is no *a priori* scheme which I can fit into. Swami Abhishiktananda underwent this excruciating and blissful experience, remaining faithful to both traditions, and he found his freedom by transcending both. But I have to tread the way myself in all sincerity, in spite of the tremendous encouragement received from him and others. My conviction is that only such an experience can really build bridges between the old and still persisting misunderstandings among the diverse spiritual traditions.

What happens when one has jumped into that melting-pot? On the one hand, my Christian faith is reduced to its essentials. After all, the fear of losing one's faith means that it has not reached the level of reality, that there is still something to be lost. It is like climbing a high mountain along a narrow path: you cannot take much baggage. First you may think that all this baggage is necessary, but higher up you realize that it is only a burden, and the lighter you walk, the easier you will reach the peak. First of all, renunciation applies not only to worldly but also to religious possessions. Secondly, in real renunciation one does not give up any real value, one only pierces to the core and so one does not feel the need for the externals any longer. In a sense I do not feel that I have lost anything, though it may appear so. On the contrary, the deep Christian archetypes reappear often in a different and unexpected context. I could cite examples from the realms of religious expression, ritual, etc., in the relation between guru and disciple, in spiritual experience or insights. For example, several times I had the experience of communion in the full sense in a Hindu context, where the participants never had any direct contact with Christ. There was no need to use the name, the spiritual reality was there. Christian churches are not yet ready for an intercommunion among themselves — but to my mind, intercommunion should go far beyond the narrow boundaries of Christianity, a real sharing of religious values in theory and practice. In fact, one of the results of an inter-religious experience is that the "names and forms" lose their importance and one necessarily becomes more attentive to the reality indicated by them. This is an exercise in sensitive awareness. This deep attentiveness leads sooner or later to a complete transcending of the names and forms, and a piercing through to what lies behind them. Is not this transcendence the very purpose of any religious expression or doctrine?

If somebody asks (or I ask myself): how can you believe in Christ and Shiva at the same time? my answer will be a further question: who is Christ? who is Shiva? and, who am I? Shiva is not a name or any mythological personality, he is the "gracious one", the great Lord *(Parameshvara)*, the ultimate Reality *(anuttara)*, the most intimate I-consciousness of every conscious being. Christ is not merely the historical personality, otherwise I would not have cared to follow him. He is "the Way, the Life and the Truth" — but not in an exclusive sense; on the contrary. Even beyond that he is essentially the "I am": "Then you will know that 'I am'." How can one limit the "I am" to only one person? Here I learn from Kashmir Shaivism or Ramana Maharshi that the ultimate "I" of every conscious being is the divine "I". The ultimate realization is not of some "objective" truth: "This is He", but the personal discovery: "I am He". In this way every spiritual practice in the inter-religious context leads to a kind of purification from mere conceptions.

The theological implications of such an experience, which is certainly not without suffering and conflict, will have to be worked out. Though such a double experience cannot be imitated or generalized, it is also far from being individualistic. Any authentic inner experience is lived in solidarity — with the church, with humanity or whatever one may call it. If it is not somehow universal or all-embracing, it cannot be called an authentic spiritual experience. Are we Christians not too much concerned with labels instead of contents? A spiritual dialogue should precisely go beyond labels — only to discover that perhaps the unknown pilgrim on the dusty and hot Indian road in whose presence we feel "our hearts burning", is in reality He, the Risen One.

* * *

In the present spiritual situation, East and West, I could perhaps define my situation by describing possible and actual positive and negative attitudes. The present meeting of spiritualities can be the greatest source of enlightenment as well as the most dangerous source of confusion and distortion. Starting with the negative:

1. I do not feel comfortable with most of the imitations of Eastern religious practices in the West. They lack the background on which those practices make sense and when superimposed on a Western psyche they can create the greatest confusion. I am not only referring to the neo-Hindu "sects" and guru-cults, but even to the grafting of such authentic traditions as Tibetan Buddhism for example on Western soil. What is required here is: (a) knowledge of the background, and (b) a kind of integration with the Western and Christian tradition. The churches are doing very little to help people in understanding and integrating such experiences.

2. I am ill at ease with fundamentalist Christians who are scared of any kind of contamination. They are not only living in an ivory tower, but are also creating a terribly distorted image of Christ and Christianity which makes a spiritual dialogue with other faiths difficult if not impossible.

3. I am also not at ease with the so-called "inculturation" of the church in India (I cannot speak about other countries), because most of the time it is only a superficial adaptation of elements of Indian traditions, just to show that "we are also Indian". No real spiritual transformation accompanies the external adaptations. Hindus are probably right in their criticism that this kind of "adaptation" is only another manifestation of the same old missionary mentality.

"Inculturation" is only authentic if it springs from a real inner need and if it is accompanied by a sincere spiritual dialogue within and without. No Hindu or Buddhist will object to an authentic spirituality, but they are very sensitive to imitations and make-believe.

4. What I find equally unsatisfactory is a syncretism which is practised mostly in Western countries where people jump from yoga to shamanism, from the Jesus prayer to Hare Krishna, from Tantric practices to Zen Buddhism, etc. It has become a kind of spiritual supermarket where one can pick and choose (and pay for it, too!), but nothing goes really deep or is carried forward in all seriousness.

Examples of possible positive attitudes are:

1. One may be a practising Christian and receive inspiration in all openness from other spiritual traditions, through books, meetings, exposure, etc.

2. One may sincerely and fully accept another spiritual tradition, without giving up one's own roots. This vocation may be rare, and it is not easy, but it can be pioneering also for others.
3. A Christian may reach a point in his or her experience where the externals of religion are transcended, and thus touch also upon the experience of other traditions. This has been called "transcending religions" in a mystical experience, where the labels do not matter any longer.

These three positive attitudes are in reality not so clearly distinguishable, because one may lead to another, yet I consider them as authentic ways of relating to other spiritualities.

Beyond Words and Logic

CHEWN JIUAN A. LEE

While Hindu spirituality has shaped the search of a number of Christians from the Indian sub-continent, and those others who came into dialogue with it, there were some at the consultation who were intensely helped by the Buddhist tradition in its many forms. Sister Agnes (Chewn Jiuan A. Lee) who had the two traditions of Christianity and Buddhism as part of her own life, told us how she discovered each one of them with the help of the other. A convert to Christianity from Buddhism, she rediscovered Buddhism in her search for authentic spiritual life as a Christian. Thinking of her own Christian life she felt that it had too many "oughts" and "shoulds" without providing concrete prescriptions to actualize them. Worship was too "wordy" and too "busy", with sometimes no silence, and certainly no way into silence.

Coming from an ordinary Chinese humanistic milieu, made up of a mixture of Confucianism, Taoism and Buddhism, in my early years of Christian life I experienced a sense of unsettledness, a feeling of something missing. I did not know how to name it. This feeling lasted for more than ten years. Finally, in the late sixties, I was able to see, for me, the inadequacy of Christian theology and spirituality. On the one hand, theologians' interpretations of Christian belief and practice now appeared to me as an intellectual game which destroyed their living essence. On the other hand, in the line of practice there were so many oughts and shoulds which did not provide concrete prescriptions to actualize them.

I encountered the lack of a consistent, "coherent", metaphysical-cosmological ground in Christian theology and in Christian spiritual practice. Also, there was no sound psychological foundation. Under these circumstances I turned to my own Chinese religious-spiritual traditions to search for a more holistic and integrated philosophy of life.

Since I found it difficult to make sense out of theology, I decided to free myself from it, i.e. not to be troubled by my inability to follow the words and logic of theology. Instead, I began to follow the direction of the Ch'an (Zen) Buddhist path to enlightenment:

> A special transmission outside the scriptures;
> No dependence upon words and letters;
> Direct pointing the heart (soul) of man;
> Seeing one's nature and attain Buddhahood.

Since then I have been perfectly content with Lao Tzu's evocative words: "The Tao that can be spoken of is not the unchanging Tao. The name that can be named is not the unchanging name."[1] These words put my mind to rest and induce a deep sense of awe from within.

> Meditation is the deliberate and usually systematic reflection on some truth or passage of scripture. It has a threefold purpose: to instruct the mind, to move the will, and to warm the heart for prayer. There is a pronounced intellectual element in meditation, and it could quite easily become just an exercise of the mind ("a preaching of a sermon to oneself" as some have described it) unless there were safeguards to direct it into the channel of prayer.[2]

The above description is typical of the understanding of meditation in the Christian tradition. However, I was no longer able to follow this practice. With some necessary adaptation, I have taken up the practice of Mahayana Ch'an (Zen) meditation and Therevada vipassana (i.e. insight, awareness) meditation. Both teach the radical simplification of the functions of our sense organs and of mental activity. It is in such state of utter simplicity that one can simultaneously experience the loss of self and the presence of the ultimate *One*.

Experience has taught me that there is a qualitative difference between Christian spiritual practice and the spiritual disciplines of other religious traditions. Of course the difference is due to the entirely different metaphysical and psychological foundations. Christian prayer for the most part remains in the dualistic realm where the experience of the ultimate *One* is rather shallow, i.e. it remains still on the level of relationships. This is precisely the problem with words, symbols and logic. In order to go beyond this stage, in addition to silent meditation I have also taken up the practice of mantra chanting.

Mantra is a short, simple repetitive form of vocal prayer, something like the Jesus prayer. Often the melody has a cyclical character which is different from the linear progressive movement in many Western musical compositions. Mantra chanting has the power to silence the mind and emotions, and eventually to enable the chanter to sink into the abyss of utter silence where the internal dialogue ceases and true prayer happens.

Since scripture reading plays an essential role in the Christian practice of meditation, in the process of my inculturation and adaptation I tried to find the underlying elements of the texts that have engendered life throughout the ages. It was through Far Eastern religious consciousness in general and the Mahayana perspective in particular that I learned to experience the scripture passages.

When we encounter any sacred scripture certain basic attitudes (or psychological dispositions) are needed:

1. The time element in the scripture for the reader is always present tense.
2. A reader must identify him/herself with the main persons in the text.
3. Jesus' personal pronoun "I" does not refer to an exclusive, separated individual, but an all-inclusive commonality, the true Self. At the same time it refers to one individual.
4. Sacred scripture is not subjected to historical analysis and intellectual speculation.

Any spiritual discipline is only a means, a finger-pointing to the moon. It should not be dogmatized or absolutized. It is to be used with freedom and detachment. The practitioner should transcend it as one grows in spiritual maturity.

NOTES

[1] *Tao Te Ching*, Ch. 1.
[2] *The Cloud of Unknowing*, trans. by Clifton Wolters, Penguin Classics, p.20.

Through Other Religious Disciplines

Again and again the participants at the consultation affirmed the value of various forms of meditation in deepening their own devotional and prayer lives. To some extent the exploration of other spiritualities resulted out of a feeling that practical advice in the discipline of prayer was for the most part lacking in the Christian tradition. While the Orthodox tradition's practice of prayer within the Christian tradition is well-known to Christians, there is apparently no access to it for ordinary non-Orthodox Christians who search for guidance in prayer.

Christians, however, seem to find guidance from the meditative practices within Buddhism and Hinduism. Since Christianity in general does not seem to provide believers with a method for the practice of prayer many have found, for example, the Zen method as something one could adopt for Christian practice. Quite a few shared with the group their experience of finding prayer within Christian tradition to be haphazard, shallow, or simply too wordy, until they had found ways of stillness, nurtured by the Eastern disciplines of meditation.

In the following three accounts we have examples of a search for a more disciplined approach to prayer which was discovered with the help of other religious disciplines.

Learning to Let Go

PASCALINE COFF, OSB

As a child born into a pious Catholic family I grew up loving devotional feasts, especially those of the Heart of Christ and the Mother of God. Eventually it became clear that all feasts were feasts of the heart. I became deeply impressed by the gift of the eucharist and began seeking communion through the sacrament daily, striving and begging to have Christ's mind and heart in me. At that time in history the Catholic Church was stressing the Real Presence, and I literally pursued this Real Presence, making visits and prayer before the sacrament at every opportunity. (The longest time without daily communion since then was during an Intermonastic Dialogue Exchange in Tibetan Monasteries, when, for three weeks we were unable to secure wine for the celebration of the mass!)

After entering monastic life — a community with a marvellous blend of devotion to the eucharist within the framework of the monastic horarium — I was sent to study St Thomas's Summa Theologica and received a PhD in theology from St Mary's, Notre Dame, before returning to my community. At this juncture I was called to be director of novices, assisting newcomers in their initial stages of monastic prayer and lifestyle.

While hungering myself for an ever deeper entrance into the inner journey, I felt doubly responsible to learn and help others on the same path (which in the early 1900s Evelyn Underhill said "begins at the top of the rough and rugged mountain of self-knowledge, but so few are willing to climb it").

I was further called to be prioress general of our monastic congregation for six years, during which time the search and hunger for inner communion increased. Taking an inventory of American spiritual resources at that time and testing some of the most promising programmes — a 30-day Ignatian retreat, centring prayer training sessions, the annual preached Benedictine retreat, a combination yoga/Zen retreat with a mantra — it became apparent that more depth and method had to be available somewhere.

It was then that Thomas Merton died in the East, opening the whole field of Eastern spirituality as a necessary complement to the West. Br David Steindl-Rast was often invited to general chapters as a spiritual resource and his message began to sound the riches of the East. After my term of office in leadership, I requested a year of prayer at a Christian/ Hindu ashram in South India, one guided by an early Benedictine monk, a graduate of Oxford who had been in India for 25 years.

The year at the ashram was all I hoped for and more. Hindu Bhakti (loving devotion) was a profound gift. The Namalvars and Tamil poets were mystical minstrels with delightful and vibrant hearts. St Augustine said: "To sing is to pray twice." At Fr Bede Griffiths' Hindu/Christian ashram bhajans began and ended meditation periods like poles holding each day in place. Christian and Hindu readings were used during the monastic office of lauds and vespers, as were sacred readings from other world religions.

The ancient Eastern fire blessing called the *arati* was used daily, as well as flowers around the eucharistic gifts. Outside the ashram in South India we were able to take in a ten-day intensive Vipassana retreat at Igot Puri in North India led by S.N. Goenka, and we visited Hindu ashrams where bhajans were sung continuously.

Our Christian monastic ashram in the Green Hills of eastern Oklahoma was founded in June 1980. Since an ashram is a place where people of all religions are welcome, a place of simple life-style and intensive spiritual practice, we have been able to incorporate many of the treasures of the East into our day.

Our monastery has symbols of other religions in the main hall and chapel so that all who come feel at home. There are statues of Buddha, Nataraj, Avalokatesvara, Tibetan thankas and rudraksha malas from Rishikesh alongside Japanese Buddhist prayer beads. On the north wall of the chapel also hangs a peace pipe and an American Indian drum.

The day begins with a bhajan at 5.45 a.m., sung by the weekly liturgy leader. After 20-30 minutes of contemplative meditation, the leader concludes the time by repeating the bhajan one more time. Morning praises follow using the Vedic experience with hymns from the Rig Veda for the invitatory with an antiphon sung from Western or Eastern scriptures. We also use bhajans during the eucharist as an alternate mode of singing hymns. It is often more suitable to sing one line again and again when it fits the theme of a feast, rather than a hymn of many stanzas that are not particularly appropriate. And, of course, repetition is the mother of learning.

Of all the hours of prayer, our noon praises are the most influenced by Eastern spirituality. We begin the time by singing the Gayatri mantra in English after a long Ommmmm, and concluding it with a long

Ommmmmmmmm. Fifteen minutes of silent meditation follow. The quiet time ends with an Eastern prayer: "Lord of the Universe, O Eternal Consciousness, Universal Lord I bow to you." The reading then is usually taken from Eastern wisdom. A time for reflection follows, then several sections of psalm 118. An oration drawn from one of the universal prayers of Hindu origin is prayed and the hour is concluded as are all others of the divine office with the universal prayer for peace.

On Sunday during our eucharist flowers are carried to the altar and placed around the gifts with invocations to Christ as Being, Consciousness and Bliss, or Jesus, Son of God, we adore you... we praise you... we worship you, and the like. The arati is used with incense around the gifts and again the flame-waving is done at the anamnesis. On Sundays and feastdays during evening vespers the arati is used at the conclusion of the hour, first being waved around the Lord who made the fire, at the tabernacle, and then it is brought by the leader to each one present, to take the flame in gesture with their hands through their eyes into the cave of their heart where the One who made the fire and is the fire is waiting, ever present, ever loving, ever burning.

During daily vespers special readings are selected from the sacred writings of other world religions. These are read as a first reading, following the theme of the second reading assigned from a Western patristic or papal source for that day. An introduction briefly points up the theme before the readings begin. On Sunday evenings we often have a Hindu professor from a nearby university who loves to come and share *satsang* (faith-sharing) and read the Eastern scripture for us during vespers.

Satsang is an ancient Hindu practice greatly revered. It is said one could expect salvation from sharing the company of the blessed or holy ones wherein the stories of the life and examples of the loving Lord are told again and again. At satsang we often request our Hindu guest and sometimes his friends to share stories from their sacred myths. This has been enriching for us as a community. The exchange has been very helpful. Sometimes it flows very easily, at other times it must be worked at.

At times we have had spiritual teachers to lead sessions or provide input on Eastern spirituality. One such "retreat" was a five-day intensive one with an eight-hour sit-in the last day. The staff has also gone out to make Christian Zen retreats elsewhere in the country.

Each afternoon at the ashram there is a one-hour period of Christian Zen or contemplative sitting, open to the public. This is led by one of the staff with some short introduction to contemplative prayer from a Christian mystic or Eastern wisdom, then a knocker (Korean temple clapper) is sounded, then three spaced strokes of cymbals or bells for all to get in place. Twenty-five minutes of quiet sitting follow with a five-minute contemplative walk before twenty-five more minutes of sitting. The chapel is so arranged that zafus and pads are available, as well as benches or large pillows for sitting. We use zen benches for worship.

While the Tibetan monks visited us from their monasteries in exile in India a few years ago, we shared dialogue sessions with them each morning and had intended to have satsang each evening. We learned quickly that in dialogue one must be sure of the terminology. Satsang for the Tibetans means "husband and wife"! At any rate, we did share our experiences each evening with the monks while they were here on the Intermonastic Hospitality Programme, phase II, sponsored by the North American Board for East-West Dialogue. One whole afternoon was devoted to prayer lectures given by the Geshi, translated by one of the younger Tibetan monks who spoke English. This was much appreciated by people in the area, together with the community and ashramites.

On another occasion we hosted Fr Bede Griffiths of South India. His satsangs too were shared with many of our neighbours and the people from Tulsa.

Coloured slides were taken of the 1986 Intermonastic Hospitality Programme, phase III, when six of us Benedictines, three monks and three nuns, journeyed to 26 Tibetan monasteries in India and four nunneries. Both here in the States and in India it was apparent that hospitality becomes the context in which communion happens. As Thomas Merton said at the first All Asian Congress for monastics, "dialogue is communication that becomes communion".

Enlightenment through Zen

THOMAS G. HAND, SJ

For almost twenty years now I have been engaged in interfaith dialogue, especially in the field of practical spirituality. I am an American Jesuit priest, and I have lived in Japan for 29 years. For six years I formally practised Zen under Yasutani Hakuun Roshi and Yamada Koun Roshi,

Kamakura. I am still doing Zazen. For the past three-and-a-half years I have been on the staff of Mercy Center, Burlingame, CA, USA, especially engaged in the programme of our Institute of Contemporary Spirituality. For example, we have directed three Buddhist-Christian dialogue conferences, entitled "The Human Path", where the accent was on practice. I regularly direct intensive meditation retreats of seven, two, and one day(s), daily morning and weekly meditation sessions. In all of these many Eastern insights and practices are incorporated into Christian practice.

My main area of study has been Mahayana Buddhism, especially Zen. I have also seriously investigated Vajrayana Buddhism and classical Taoism (Lao Tzu and Chuang Tzu). At the recent Buddhist-Christian conference at Berkeley I presented a paper on "A Study on the Possible Impact of Mahayana Consciousness on the Christian Doctrine of the Personal God". It is against this background that the following practices are to be seen.

Beginning with the external and bodily, the main place of most of our meditations here at Mercy Center is the Rose Room (so called because the unfolding rose is the symbol of enlightenment in the West just as the lotus is in the East). On the walls are Japanese *shikishi* (fine paper squares) with Zen sayings in Sino-Japanese ideographs, two Taoist paintings and a picture of the Miroku Bosatsu (Maitreya Bodhisattva) from Koryuji, Kyoto. These are well received by people and set a good tone to the room. However, the main shrine or centrepiece has, of course, the cross as central. It is hoped that before too long this cross will give way to a statue of Christ seated in meditation, a statue which will include clear influence from Buddhist statuary in its simplicity and feeling.

During meditation people can sit on chairs or prayer seats, but zafu (Zen prayer cushions) are the most used. The lines of meditators do not face the shrine but are in Rinzai style, facing one another. The bells and the wooden drum *(mokugyo)* are all from Buddhist shops. We use a lot of bows and also do walking meditation like the Zen *kinhin*. We have found that very few people, if any, are disturbed by all of this. Rather, they are helped by the quiet, meditative atmosphere produced by it.

Another area in which other faith influence is apparent is in our chanting. We chant briefly at the beginning of meditation periods, in order to bring our energies together and to create that special silence that arises after chanting. We use the sacred syllable *Om* in itself and also join it to the Hebrew names of Mary and Jesus *(Om Miriam, Om Jeshua)*. At first glance this may seem like a hybrid, but actually it turns out to be an excellent chant. Also, one of the ways we chant *Halleluia* has a definitely Jewish feel to it. Then, following the way some Americans (trained in Korean Zen) chant the *Heart Sutra* in English, we chant the 27th psalm in English to the beat of the *mokugyo*. Finally, we have put Latin words to a Chinese Pure Land Buddhist chant and it works very well both while seated and while walking. The words used are "Jesu Christ, salva nos" (Jesus Christ, save us, or make us whole).

The policy that we follow in leading meditation is that, while people are expected to go along together in the externals, they are free to do any interior practice they wish. The result is that during any given sitting, one person might be doing a Christian visualization, another might be reciting a mantra (Christian or not), another could be using a vipassana or vajrayana meditation method, and so on. When actually directing people on which meditation method to adopt, I try to fit the method to the experience and actual state of each individual. In the variety of meditation practices that I draw from when directing people there is obviously influence from both Christian and Buddhist traditions.

Some people do best with a Zen-like attention to their breathing, with or without counting. It is surprising how many find this to be their basic practice. Quite a number use a mantra, either Christian or otherwise. Some of the vipassana methods (for example, those given in De Mello's *Sadhana*) are sometimes used. From Hinduism I have taken some basic teaching and practice built around the energy centres *(chakras)* and both direct people individually in certain practices and also direct whole groups in some simple exercises. One practice that some, including myself, do quite frequently is to go up the chakras chanting from each centre (usually interiorly) the beja or seed mantra for each centre together with the name Miriam. Thus: Lam Miriam, Vam Miriam, Ram Miriam, Jam Miriam, Ham Miriam, Om Miriam, and Aum Miriam. Since Miriam is the archetype of openness to the Holy Spirit, this is done to purify and open out each chakra and in effect one's whole self. Then one goes down the seven centres chanting from each one the beja mantras and the sacred name, Jeshua. This is done to anoint the centres and one's whole self with the Holy Spirit. In conclusion one can return to the ajna (command) centre in the forehead and remain there chanting *Om Jeshua*. I have also worked out a seemingly valid and genuine correlation between the seven petitions of the Our Father and the seven chakras. It is a fine way of reciting this fundamental prayer; and since each of us is a mini human race and a mini cosmos, used with this thought it becomes a prayer over not only oneself but also over the whole world and the cosmos.

One basic prayer form that I came to through Zen is pure attention or objectless, formless prayer. In Japanese Zen it is called *shikan taza* ("nothing but applying oneself to sitting"). From Zen practice I became convinced that this is true prayer and now direct people to it with confidence. In shikan taza that which is attentive is the heart of the person. The other powers of attention are basically quiet (the senses, imagination, intellect). We all admit that we have a heart, but where and what is it? In fact, it is nowhere and outside all categories. It is the infinite dimension of the human being. It is the power by which we know God. As Augustine said, our hearts are intrinsically oriented towards the experience of God, "our hearts are made for Thee, O God..." Therefore prayer is simply letting the heart take its natural course. Prayer is attention of the heart and the focus of this attention is the formless Infinite. This is meditation without a focused object. For those trained in traditional Western methods of Christian prayer assurance must usually be given that it is all right to just sit, that devotional thought and emotion are not essential to true prayer. It has proved helpful to give even a brief presentation of the teaching of *The Cloud of Unknowing* and/or some other representative of the apophatic tradition within Christianity. As I see it, "the naked stirring of the heart", which is the basic prayer of the author of *The Cloud,* is truly the same thing as shikan taza. Standing upon a "cloud of forgetting", which means putting aside all thoughts and concepts, even the thought of "the Lord Jesus and his blessed passion", one stands looking up to the "cloud of unknowing" with nothing but this "naked stirring of the heart".

To my mind there is one point where Zen and the East in general are more helpful and more in touch with the actual movement of the Spirit within people. *The Cloud* demands years of training and practice of discursive prayer, together with certain clear signs, before a person can take up this "prayer of the heart". The tradition in the East is more for early and free entry into formless prayer for all who feel its attraction. I have followed this line and have found a surprising number who move easily into such meditation.

Another area in which Zen has given clarity regarding meditation and other spiritual practices is in the question of motivation. Christians are often directed to more rectitude, to peace in one's daily life and especially to ministry for others as the goal of spiritual practices. While not rejecting any such fruits in any way, Zen is very clear and simple. We meditate in order to come to enlightenment. Although in my own life and in the direction of others I put enlightenment in largely Christian terms (to share in the self-identification of Christ Jesus or to experience the oneness of all in God or the Christ-consciousness or the discovery of the Christ-self), nevertheless I do follow Buddhism in the simplicity and clarity of its motivation. This is the reason behind the name Rose Room we have given to our meditation room.

I have not gone into the Buddhist influence I have experienced in the whole area of scripture study, theology and general philosophy of life. For example, because of Buddhism I have come to take very seriously the infinity of God and the true meaning of Absolute (and relative). This has had profound effect on both my thinking and practice.

A Search for Spiritual Roots

PETER K.H. LEE

A third-generation Chinese Christian from Hong Kong, I grew up in the Anglican church, where as a youth I sang in the choir. I learned to like the liturgical music and worship of the church and, through my mother, who was an active churchwoman, I came to appreciate the importance of church fellowship.

I went to an English school which had a colonial flavour. The family was fortunate to have a Mandarin-speaking tutor, coming out of the Cultural Renaissance Movement (1919), who reminded me of my Chinese cultural heritage (which must be renewed in every generation). My American-educated father thought that science and democracy offered the best hope for China. At the same time he loved to tell stories from Chinese history to his children.

I entered college in the United States, first to study science, but later expanded my interest to cover humanistic studies, graduating with a degree in philosophy. I thus had a really good liberal arts education in the Western tradition. One of the courses I liked, however, was on world religions.

My decision to enter the Christian ministry came after some struggles on two fronts: (1) I was not satisfied with Anglican formalism and clericalism (but retained my love for its liturgical music), and I was drawn to the personal warmth of Wesleyan piety; (2) I went along with the Methodist interest in social issues, yet I felt something missing until, thanks to a lecture on John Wesley, I learned that for him divine grace runs through justification, sanctification and social action, while human efforts are assumed. Upon graduation from seminary I was ordained in the United Methodist Church.

After a few years of pastoral experience (in multi-racial congregations in California and Hawaii), I went for further graduate studies in theology. I ended up with a doctorate in ecumenics and world religions.

I felt the call to return to Hong Kong. That was twenty years ago. First in the pastorate and then in the university setting, I continued to be spiritually dissatisfied. I sensed, moreover, that my Western theological background and American church orientation made me a stranger in my homeland. Hong Kong, to be sure, is a British colony, with a capitalist economic system brought from abroad, plenty of foreign-made consumer goods flooding the market, and life-styles copied from the West. But beneath the surface there are Chinese characteristics, which have religious-cultural roots. Besides, Hong Kong is adjacent to China which, although it has undergone political and social convulsions in recent decades, remains the homeland of a people with a long civilization.

In my youth, one of the subjects which fascinated me was projective geometry. In doing projective geometry, one works on a mathematical equation and then projects on a piece of paper a geometrical shape. The algebraic equation uses highly abstract symbols to work out a mathematical problem. Now the geometrical lines and shapes are objects projected on a piece of paper external to the mind. The way projective geometry works symbolizes the typical mode of thinking in Western science and philosophy. The thinking subject, the mind, is separate from the object of thought (which is highly abstract), and if in some mysterious way there is a kind of correspondence between the subject and thought, an equation consisting of abstract symbols serves as a key. In Western thought, this subject-object dichotomous mode of thinking has aided the expansion of scientific ("objective") knowledge and the advancement of modern technology (by efficiently manipulating material "objects"). But it is emotionally and spiritually impoverishing.

Apply the subject-object bifurcation of reality to human beings and social relations and God, and you miss out the vital elements. At the risk of gross over-simplification, in this I see the crux of much dissatisfaction of the human spirit and the disarray of society in modern Western civilization. (If I am not mistaken, René Descartes, who made the expression *cogito ergo sum* immortal, was one of the innovators of projective geometry, but I do not want to blame him for all the troubles of the Western world.) In the subject-object scheme I recognize the limitations of much of Western theological works — and of church life in the West too.

There was no "sudden awakening" in me, but the subject-object dualism has been mended over the years. One of the tonics which have been helpful is the enjoyment of Chinese scroll painting (or "mountain and water painting"), which shows the influence of the Taoist spirit. The spirit of Tao flows ever so subtly: typically, as in a Chinese painting, it allows the mountain, the stream, the sky, the horizon, the trees, etc. to merge into one another; and where a person (invariably a tiny figure) is present, it is through him that consciousness of the Tao is gently enhanced. The onlooker of the painting is drawn into the picture through the consciousness of the tiny figure in contemplation of the scenery. Unfortunately I do not paint, but I collect Chinese scroll paintings (reproductions), and it is a pleasure to look at them.

The Chinese poetical world also breathes the spirit of Tao. What an infinitely greater delight it is to read Chinese poetry than Western theological treatises! To be sure, substantive theological works provide food for thought. Yet many a lyrical Chinese poem is rich in spiritual meaning, and it is a nectar which delights and quenches. (One of the minor projects I am undertaking is to collect poems which have a touch of Zen.) Now that I have read a good deal of Chinese poetry, I can no longer approach Christian theological subjects in the same way as before.

Speaking of Zen, let me now make mention of Zazen (*tso-ch'an* in Chinese). Zen (or *ch'an*), by the way, is a happy marriage between Taoism and Buddhism. Zazen (meaning "to sit in meditation") is a way of meditation or contemplation (some experts make a distinction between the two, but I shall not bother to do so) which finally leads to formlessness, detachment, emptiness and receptivity. Typically, Zazen starts out by concentrating on breathing or an object, but eventually it enters into a formless state of consciousness. I have not practised Zazen persistently and I am without a good *roshi,* yet I have done enough on my own to realize inner unbound space, which is a totally different realm from the world of frantic activities and compulsive behaviour, conflicts and turmoils. Curiously, from a sea of stillness, so to speak, eventually flow energy, creativity and empathy with the world at large. I have barely had a taste of contemplative practice and I would like to explore it further and seek counsel from others who are more experienced and adept at it.

Furthermore, I would like to link it to Christian spirituality. One of the effects one gains from Zen is freeing oneself from fixation of any kind, yet there is an inherent spiritual power in those touched by Zen, and the spirituality here can be incorporated into Christian living.

We should also mention Christian spiritual exercises where meditation is a directed course of predominantly intellectual activity, dwelling upon ideas with specific Christian contents. I refer to the practice of meditating on a selected scriptural passage, on a certain episode in the life of Jesus, or a symbol. I can appreciate the value of this kind of meditation whereby one interiorizes an externally given form, or relates one's experience to it, until one's subjectivity is absorbed by the object.

In reviewing what I have written so far, I recall a three-way classification of meditation I came across some time ago. I still keep a copy of the chart,[1] which is reproduced here.

The negative way:
elimination, detachment, emptiness;
centred

The way of forms:
concentration and absorption;
outer-directed

The expressive way:
freedom and transparency;
inner-directed

Zazen is a notable model of the Negative Way. Chinese scroll painting and poetry are illustrations of the Expressive Way. Traditional Christian meditation (using a scriptural passage or a symbol) is an instance of the Way of Forms. Can these three ways be creatively integrated?

Whether it is Taoist and Buddhist meditation, or Christian spirituality for that matter, there is the temptation to be contented with one's own wellbeing primarily, leaving a concern for others as a secondary matter.

It is Confucian ethical teachings which have impressed upon me the great importance of moral development. To be sure, much of what may be called Confucianism we see in Chinese society (in Hong Kong, Taiwan and other communities) nowadays is institutionalized and without life. But I was determined to go back to the classical texts, and whenever possible I would talk to persons in whom Confucian teachings come alive. I am sure that people who have the quality of *jen* (benevolence or human-heartedness) are as morally excellent as any group of human beings can be. If Confucianism is ethical humanism par excellence, it is not without reference to the transcendent (*tien*, "heaven"), and spiritually reverberates with morality. The late Thomé Fang put it, thinking of Confucianism especially: "The development of Chinese spirituality culminates in the perfection of ethical culture." [2] This is a powerful reminder to me that spirituality has moral contents.

Another potent reminder to me that the spiritual person has moral qualities is the Bodhisattva ideal of Mahayana Buddhism. The Bodhisattva vows to postpone his/her entrance into Nirvana until he/she finishes the mission of saving suffering sentient beings. The Bodhisattva ideal is meant to supplement the Theravada Buddhist ideal of Arahat, who is concerned primarily about his own spiritual wellbeing. I am not satisfied with talk of an ideal only; I would like to see ethical values translated into practical terms. Once, after witnessing a "creatures-freeing" ceremony in a Buddhist temple, I asked a nun there if the ceremony had important practical implications for people today. At first she replied that the ceremony was symbolic, but she later admitted that a Buddhist should live his/her life just as the ceremony suggests — always be ready to free living creatures from bondage. On another occasion I talked with a Buddhist monk about the Eightfold Noble Path, and I was impressed by the seriousness with which he adhered to the Right View, Right Speech, Right Efforts, etc. He would make the Right Efforts to improve his moral character; he would also like to see that others do the same. And he lamented the laxity of morality in the *sangha* nowadays.

Social justice is an essential component of divine love. It is strongly emphasized by the Old Testament prophets. Social justice is not stressed in Taoism or Buddhism; it is implied in Confucian ethical teachings but it needs to be developed. Christians have often forgotten the theme of social justice. In my own case, it is partly by listening to the Marxist critique of capitalist society that I gain a renewed understanding of the urgency of social justice; also, exposure to social realities has helped to conscientize me to the same end. I now feel more strongly than ever that a spirituality which has no sense of social justice is emaciated.

Social justice is not just a matter of talking or thinking, but it involves action, even community action. Spirituality is often conceived of in terms of contemplation and prayer. But we have just said that social justice is an essential dimension of spiritual life. Where, then, do we see the interface between contemplation and action?

As a matter of fact, "contemplation and action" are spoken of by more and more people nowadays in one breath. I value the contemplative temperament when I see activists who run around in all directions without knowing why and without finding a bearing. I am attracted to the contemplative life in that it takes time to be with God in silence, and seeks reflection and growth in spiritual wisdom. Yet for all intents and purposes, very few can cut themselves off from the bustle of the world. Indeed, when we are confronted by the social realities of injustice, oppression and exploitation, we cannot sit still all day long, but must feel it part of our responsibility to do something to alleviate the pain of people.

All through Chinese intellectual history the theme of "unity of thought and action" appears again and again. It is an accepted norm in Chinese culture, reinforced by Confucian thought especially, that educated persons assume responsibility for establishing the public good. To be sure this norm or ideal does not always work out right. Still, it is not something that I would disregard hastily. Off and on I find myself considering the issue of relating the ideal to the practical world. In the Neo-Confucianist philosopher Wang Yang-Ming (1472-1529), for instance, I see flashes of insight, approaching the issue from epistemological, ethical, and metaphysical perspectives.

One more subject I wish to bring up is the ecological crisis in the modern age. The teachings of Lao-Tzu and Taoist-influenced paintings have been helpful in restoring my sense of communion with nature. As a result, I now approach the biblical doctrine of creation with enhanced appreciation. Restoring a personal sense of wholeness in relation to the created order, however, is one thing; it is something else to mobilize efforts to overcome the present ecological crisis, using science and technology and human resources to create a living environment more in harmony with God's will. To be able to fashion a material and human world in close cooperation with God is another important item on the agenda of our search for a contemporary spirituality.

By now I feel quite at home in the Chinese religious-cultural milieu. Chinese philosophy and religion, generally speaking, lead to a sense of harmony of things, and this is a needed remedy for Western culture, which breeds fragmentation and disjointedness. Due to the "fallenness" of humanity, however, the world is full of conflicts. Chinese religiosity and wisdom can hardly cope with such a world. Traditional Christian spirituality is quite helpless too in the face of the hard realities of the world. But the heart of the Christian message is precisely that God in Christ reconciles the world to God. Again and again I return to the cross as the focal point of reconciliation between God and fallen humanity and the world. Certainly there is deep spirituality here. Thus, indeed, the whole sweep of biblical revelation becomes vibrant with life for me — from God's creation to the covenant with God's people, from the Old Testament prophets' pronouncements to the life and teachings of Jesus, and finally to Jesus' death and resurrection.

NOTES

[1] Claudio Naranjo and Robert E. Ornstein, *On the Psychology of Meditation,* London, George Allen & Unwin Ltd, 1972, p.16.
[2] Thomé H. Fang, *The Chinese View of Life,* Hong Kong, Union Press, 1969, pp.42-43.

The World of Spiritual Discoveries

MARY O. DRISCOLL, OP

"My interest in and the enrichment that has come to me from the practices of other faiths", says Mary O'Driscoll, "are the result of a number of diverse experiences I have had at different times and in different places during my life." Born in Ireland, O'Driscoll grew up with no contact whatever with persons of other faiths. She had known that there was a Jewish community in Ireland but had no contact with them. As for the other religions, she had never heard of them. Once exposed to them she found enormous riches that she could own.

Being Irish by birth and upbringing, in my years of adolescence I grew up far removed from persons of other faiths, and consequently knew almost nothing about them or their practices. True, there is a small number of Jewish people living in Ireland, but I had no contact with them. And, as far as Buddhists, Hindus and Muslims were concerned, I had scarcely even heard of them!

It was in my early adult life when, having joined the Dominican Order, I went as a missionary to South Africa that I had my first exposure to other faiths. Here I encountered and worked closely both with black Africans and with Muslims, neither of whom shared my Christian faith but rather lived in two other deeply religious worlds of their own. I spent over 15 years in Africa and learnt much from my interfaith contacts there, which has continued to enrich me.

Since 1975, when I left South Africa, I have been fortunate enough, through my work in the fields of spirituality and ecumenism, to visit many parts of the world and to meet a variety of people of other faiths. I can honestly say that every meeting has been instructive and helpful. I cannot recall an occasion when I did not come away enriched in some way from my interfaith exposure and dialogue. This is particularly true in the case of my contacts with Muslims in Turkey, Indonesia and Africa; and with Buddhists in Thailand, Indonesia and the United States.

Besides the understanding and appreciation of other faiths that have come to me from actual contact with members of these faiths, I have also received many insights into the great mystical traditions of Asia, and particularly of Buddhism, through my study of and teaching courses on Meister Eckhart, the fourteenth-century Rhineland mystic. He was a Dominican, and so am I, and he belongs to the period of Western spirituality with which I am most familiar, and in the area of which I teach one or two courses every year. It is generally agreed that of all the Western mystics, Meister Eckhart is the one whose thought bears most resemblance to many of the core ideas expressed in the Buddhist scriptures. Often Buddhist writings have helped me to understand Eckhart better, just as Eckhart's writings have helped me to get new insights into Buddhist teaching. This has not remained merely on the intellectual level for me but has also helped me to live out my own Christian and Dominican spirituality. Another of my favourite fourteenth-century mystics, with whose spirituality I feel very comfortable, is the Italian Dominican woman, Catherine of Siena. Her writings have shed light for me on, and given me a greater practical appreciation of, certain Buddhist meditation practices.

So, with this short personal introduction, I shall try now to respond to the question which is the focus of this paper, viz. "How are you practising your Christian spirituality adopting practices from other faiths?"

Firstly, I would say that my knowledge and experience of Buddhism have affected how I prepare for prayer and even, in some sense, how I pray. I find that one of the best ways for me to enter into a prayerful, recollected mood is to adopt a semi-lotus position. I say "semi-lotus" because I am not able to get into the full lotus position! However, I do try to approximate it in some way according to my actual circumstances at the time of prayer. This position wards off for me two particular dangers which rear their heads when the time of prayer comes round: (1) the danger of assuming a position which is so comfortable that it lulls me to sleep or at least sends me into dreamland; (2) the danger of assuming a position that is so uncomfortable that I can't get past thinking about my body and how uncomfortable it is! The semi-lotus position, on the other hand, keeps me alert yet relaxed. It is thus a freeing prayer position for me.

Once in this prayer posture, I try to enter into myself through a process of becoming aware successively of my body and its physical sensations, my present emotions and feelings, and the various thoughts and ideas that are flowing through my mind. I do not attempt to judge or control any of these; rather I just stay with them, aware that they are part of who I am at the moment, until they cease to demand attention. I have discovered that this preparation for prayer which incorporates not only the Buddhist posture but also the Buddhist meditation technique of living fully in the now, has with practice become relatively easy for me, and that it is a gentle, peaceful way into prayer which suits my temperament. It helps me to get in touch with the deepest places within myself, and consequently to be aware of God within me. Catherine of Siena compares the process of entering into oneself and of discovering God at the source of one's being to the process of digging a well. She explains that just as when making a well one has to dig through much soil before one reaches running water, so we have to work through the soil of self, i.e. the false self with its deceit, duplicity and pretences, in order to reach our true self in God at the bottom of the well. This practice of dropping down into my well until I come to the place of living water, to the God of love within me, is one that I like to use. While it differs in its relational aspect from the Buddhist centring technique, it has still much in common with it. Catherine teaches that when we reach our true self in God we discover that we are nothing (God actually tells her: "You are she who is not"). There are obvious links between this teaching and the Buddhist emphasis on our nothingness.

Although Buddhists do not speak of discovering God within, and still less of being called to divinization, they do speak of finding the Buddha within and of being called to become Buddha. The Sutra of Wei Lang states:

> Within our mind there is a Buddha, and that Buddha within is the real Buddha. If Buddha is not to be sought within our mind, where shall we find the real Buddha? Doubt not that a Buddha is within your mind, apart from which nothing can exist.

What the Buddhist text says about the Buddha within with whom eventually a person is to be identified is very like what we as Christians say about the indwelling of the Trinity in us (John 14:23), and about our Christian vocation not only to be like Christ, but to be Christ (Gal. 2:20; 3:27). Recently, I came into touch with this Buddhist teaching in a very practical way. I was visiting the Buddhist commune, the Santi Asoke sangha outside Bangkok, where a kind of Buddhist "aggiornamento" is taking place. Looking around, I saw no statue or image of the Buddha anywhere. Enquiring about this, I was told that the absence of statues out there, on pedestals in temples, or in shrines in one's hut, encourages the monks and all who live in the commune to seek the Buddha within themselves. This experience helped me in trying to live St Paul's statement: "I live not now, but Christ lives in me" (Gal. 2:20).

As Christians, we all are aware of the necessity of interior silence for contemplative prayer. I have learnt much about the value of inner silence from the Buddhist practice of meditation which aims at putting a person into a state of intense and at the same time relaxed, alertness, in which he or she can be luminously and quietly present. This state of relaxed, intense alertness is for me as a Christian a state of openness and receptivity towards God. One of the Old Testament texts which is used by Eckhart to stress the necessity of interior silence, if the word of God is to be born in us, is one that appeals to me: "When all was still in the middle of the night and a gentle silence enveloped all, your all-powerful Word leaped down from heaven" (Wis. 18:14). Eckhart describes the state of interior silence as a state of "potential receptivity". Buddhists would agree with this.

I would like to share with you an exercise I sometimes use to help me into a state of interior silence. It is called "the Temple of Silence" and has the following steps:

Imagine a hill covered with greenery. A path leads to the top where you can see the Temple of Silence. Give that temple the share of your higher consciousness, noble, harmonious and radiant. Approach the top of the hill and the entrance to the temple, slowly. Ageless stillness pervades the atmosphere of the Temple of Silence... You enter the temple. You feel the atmosphere of stillness and peace all around you. Now you walk forward into the silence... you see a big, luminous dome. Its luminosity not only comes from the rays of the sun, but also seems to spring from within... You enter the luminous silence and feel absorbed by it. Let this silence pervade you. Feel it flowing through your veins and permeating every cell in your body. Listen to it; remain in it...

This exercise, which for some time now has been helpful to me in creating an atmosphere of inner silence, has taken on even more significance since I spent a short time at a Buddhist monastery in Indonesia. This monastery, which is situated in Yogyakarta in central Java, has the simplest temple I have ever seen. When I entered this temple its ambience of silence was so pervasive that it seemed to absorb me, envelop and caress me, penetrating the most hidden recesses of my being. When I left that temple I carried its silence with me for a long time. Now, whenever I do the above exercise as a preparation for prayer, it is that small, silent, Buddhist temple in central Java which comes before my mind and which helps me to be peaceful and quiet.

I have also received help for my prayer life from Islam. Perhaps the most important thing I have learned is that, while it is important to live in God's presence all the time, it is good and necessary to stop and turn deliberately towards God at certain times in the day. I am always impressed by the devout Muslim's fidelity to this practice. In Indonesia and elsewhere I discovered that even restaurants and bars have a prayer room so that Muslims can pray to Allah at the appointed times. While the Muslim turns towards Mecca in prayer, I will want to turn towards the God within me. My study of Islamic mysticism, Sufism, has shown me how much it has in common with Christian mysticism. It speaks beautifully of the same self-surrender to God in love which our Christian mystics talk about. Not only do I feel at home reading the Sufi texts, but they also encourage me to try to be more self-surrendered in love to the God of love.

In their turn, the African religions call me to a spirituality that is down to earth. They remind me that my encounter with God takes place, first of all, on this earth and not outside it. As an African author puts it: "African spirituality is a spirituality of flesh and blood." That, of course, is the message of the incarnation.

Besides the strictly prayer dimension of my Christian spirituality, other dimensions also have been greatly enriched by my contact with people and practices of other faiths. I shall mention just a few examples.

In Istanbul a few years ago, a devout Muslim, with whom I had a long conversation, explained to me that all Muslims are expected to give one-tenth of their income to the poor every year. And they are expected to do this, not in a general or impersonal way, but by taking the trouble to find out who in their locality is in need, and then by giving secretly, without any ostentation, whatever help they can to those needy persons. Since then, my religious community has tried to take this Muslim practice as a standard for our own sharing with the poor.

In South Africa recently, one of my Dominican sisters was imprisoned in solitary confinement simply because she intervened when she saw a police officer beating up a small black boy for no other reason than that he was black. She became just one of the hundreds of political prisoners who are languishing for years in the prisons of South Africa. She might have remained in prison for years, too, except that a few weeks after her arrest a group of Muslim lawyers heard of her case, and, moved by the injustice of her imprisonment, offered to bring her case to court and to defend her, free of charge. Muslims are classified as "non-white" and are consequently regarded as second-class citizens in apartheid South Africa. It was a heroic action, therefore, for these Muslim lawyers to attempt to defend a white person before a white judge. But they did it, and against all the odds, Sister Clare was freed. That Muslim example of heroic charity has affected not only me, but my whole community, and has encouraged us to be more courageous in sticking our necks out beyond the barriers of race and religion in our struggle for justice in South Africa and elsewhere.

The compassion for all who suffer which Buddhism teaches is so deep and non-discriminatory that it shows up my own acts of compassion as very small. I have been helped consequently by reading and trying to put into practice the "Four Sublime States" described in the Brahma Viharas. In loose translation, these are the states of benevolence, love, joyous sympathy and equanimity. In each of these states one is called to identify oneself with all creatures and to pervade the entire universe with thoughts of compassion "with heart grown great, wide, deep, boundless, purified of all ill-will".

From my contact with Buddhists and by observing how they put it into practice, I have learnt greater tolerance towards others, no matter how different from myself they may be.

A short while ago I read an article which explained the "seven steps to reconciliation" practised in a Buddhist monastery whenever there is need for two monks to settle a dispute that has arisen between them. It struck me that these seven steps could be very helpful in my own religious community, as well as in society in general. The steps are:

1) face-to-face sitting: in the presence of the whole sangha the feuding monks sit and face each other in silence;
2) remembrance: each monk recalls all the circumstances surrounding the dispute;
3) non-stubbornness: both are asked to be willing to be reconciled;
4) covering mud with straw: in the presence of all, one respected senior monk speaks on behalf of the two monks; the aim here is to help one side to be sympathetic towards the other; the mud is the dispute; the straw is the loving-kindness and the Dharma;
5) voluntary confession: each monk humbly reveals one or two of his weaknesses;
6) decision by consensus: the whole community decides how reconciliation can best be achieved;

7) acceptance of the verdict: both monks accept what has been decided.

Perhaps the area in which my Christian spirituality has been most influenced by the spirituality of another faith is connected with the non-possessiveness that is counselled by the gospel. Buddhist monastic teaching emphasizes that the way to enlightenment is through a detached, non-possessive attitude towards created things. It has prescriptions against hoarding what one does not need, and against an acquisitive spirit. It stresses that attachment to material goods is an insurmountable deterrent to Nirvana. All this, of course, is taught by Jesus in the gospel. The pages of scripture contain many exhortations against being possessive or putting one's happiness in material things, and about seeking the one thing necessary (cf. Matt. 6:19-34; Luke 10:41-42; 12:16-21).

When I visited the Buddhist Santi Asoke commune outside Bangkok, what struck me most forcibly was the extremely simple life-style, not only of the monks, but of all who lived there (including the governor of Bangkok who is a member of the commune). The members share everything they have with one another and with others; the little hut in the grounds in which each person or family group lives is small and almost bare, containing only the most essential necessities of life; the common meditation place is not a grand temple but an open barn-like structure; the community eats only once a day, and then very simply. I was impressed by the joy of all whom I met, young and old. The whole set-up recalled for me the way of life of the first Christians as it is described in the Acts of the Apostles (2:44-47; 4:34-35), and encouraged me to simplify my own life-style so that I could be a better witness to the gospel. All this has particular relevance for me as a Dominican. St Dominic founded the Order to preach the good news of salvation. He asked his followers to be itinerant preachers not tied down by possessions which would prevent them from moving freely from place to place. I received courage in trying to live out this vocation from my visit to the Santi Asoke commune.

As I think is obvious, I have discovered that beyond all our differences, we who are Buddhists, Muslims, Africans and Christians, have very much in common, and that by being open to the best in one another's teachings and practices we can all learn how to live our own particular spirituality at a deeper level.

Living Dialogue

YOHAN DEVANANDA

The practice of spirituality does not simply mean the use of spiritual disciplines like prayer, meditation, yoga, etc. to deepen one's awareness of oneself and the other. Even though this particular consultation was meant to help discover the issues involved in adopting or using spiritual disciplines across religious barriers, the underlying understanding of spirituality was one that affirmed the importance of participation in the historical realities of our world. Often, it was said, as one grows in one's spiritual life one is made more and more aware of the problems of the world, and also discovers a solidarity with people of other faiths in the option for the poor. Very often one discovered that a fellow pilgrim of another spiritual tradition shared the same concern for justice and peace.

Yohan Devananda from the Devasarana community in Sri Lanka, a community oriented to Christian-Buddhist-Marxist dialogue, witnesses to a new spirituality that emerges as a result of working and struggling together on common issues and problems. At the worship at Kyoto we celebrated The New World Liturgy, *a worship resource developed by Devasarana using hymns, readings and affirmations from the many religious and ideological traditions. Yohan Devananda's experience elicited from many others in the group the shared conviction that spirituality cannot be divorced from the world of action and social change.*

Many individuals, organizations and traditions have contributed to the formation of Devasarana but, essentially, it has been a dialogue and action movement with the people of Sri Lanka, rooted in the soil and culture of the land that has, under God and according to Dharma, made Devasarana what it is.

Origins

The origin was monastic and drew inspiration from the Christian tradition as well as from the traditions of the other ancient religions. In the Christian monastic tradition St Anthony of the desert and St Benedict, great founders and pathfinders, were an inspiration. St Anthony demonstrated the call to wholehearted renunciation: "Let no one who hath renounced the world think that he hath given up some great thing... the whole earth set over against heaven's infinite is scant and poor." And St Benedict was the great organizer, with his humanist ideal of a balance of prayer, study and manual labour, enshrined in a fully articulated Rule.

Ashrama and arama traditions

Then there were the ashrama and arama traditions:[1] the Hindu search for the ultimate reality through intense spiritual activity or, rather, intense "essential activity" and experience of divine powers and the Buddhist path to an awakened and liberated mind, combined with a rigorous dedication to self-control and discipline. These, too, were sources of inspiration. Through dialogue and interaction with these sources the Christian sources could be renewed and made relevant. Christian tradition has been diluted by an inter-mixture of certain aspects of modern Western tradition so that the Christian religion was being presented as a way of "getting on". Getting back to the sources of a creative renunciation common to all religions was an essential part of measuring up to the challenge of making a creative response, in depth, to the degeneration of true values under the impact of a rampant materialism.

The Italian Jesuit, Roberto D'Nobili, attempted to fuse Eastern and Western traditions in founding a Christian ashram in Madurai, South India, in the seventeenth century. This did not survive beyond D'Nobili himself, partly due to opposition from church authorities. But it was a notable effort which had an impact on the church and still remains an inspiration.

Then, early in the twentieth century, the idea was revived and the Bengalee Brahmin Christian, Brahmabandhab Upadhyaya, founded a Christian ashram on the banks of the Narbada river in North India. He prophesied that the "Christian revelation will put forth newer harmonies and newer beauties" when nurtured "in Indian soil". He also took an active part in the Indian freedom movement and died in prison but the example of his life and mission still lives.

Next, Dr Jesudasan and Dr Paton founded the Christa Kula ashram at Tirupattur in South India in 1915. In the next thirty years such ashrams were founded in many parts of India. The Christian ashram movement has played a pioneering role in the indigenization of the church in India. The pioneer of this movement in Sri Lanka was Sevak S. Selvaratnam, who founded the Christa Seva ashram in Chunnakam in the north of Sri Lanka in a Hindu context, in 1939.

Devasarana was heir to all this. The proud humility of the medieval Christian scholar comes to mind: "We are dwarfs but we stand on the shoulders of giants!" Also, the biblical injunction: "Look to the rock from which you were hewn, to the quarry from which you were dug" (Isa. 51:1). The Devasarana Movement started with the founding of Devasaranaramaya at Heyadiwela in 1957. It moved to its present site in Ibbagamuwa in 1960. This is in the north-western province of Sri Lanka in a living Buddhist environment. It is also in the Kurunegala diocese of the church of Ceylon (Anglican).

The "Aramaya" idea came out of the recognition that the church was still too much dominated by the Westernized, English-speaking elite of the towns and too cut-off from the ordinary Sinhala and Tamil-speaking people in the villages. Devananda was one of a group reflecting on this alienation. There had been, as mentioned earlier, a significant movement of indigenization of the church but it was felt that it had to go still further if it was to realize a deeper potential.

Before moving to Ibbagamuwa from Hevadiwela, Devananda spent a year in India, exploring the ashrams and holy places of India. The impact of ancient India was deep and unforgettable. But most memorable of all was his association with the Saccidananda (Shantivanam) ashram on the banks of the Kaveri river at Kulittalai, near Tiruchirapalli in South India, founded in the early 1950s by Swami Parama Arubi Anandam and Swami Abhishiktananda and stayed a month there with Swami Abhishiktananda. They continued to correspond for many years after that.

Ibbagamuwa, where the Aramaya moved to, is a remote village in the interior of Sri Lanka. Here an action-reflection movement was set in motion in the context of a Buddhist-Christian dialogue, which later developed into a Buddhist-Christian-Marxist dialogue. But in the early years there was a special emphasis on the contemplative aspect. The action dimension was primary but, at the beginning, this was mainly seen in the action of getting rooted in a village context and sharing the way of life of village people. However, the contemplative aspect was dominant and was a very important part of the initial evolution. The life at Devasarana was steeped in prayer and ascetic disciplines, drawn from both Eastern and Western traditions. This meant that any visible development was very slow, though rich in purposive contemplation.

Alongside the people

However, getting alongside people at the grassroots and sharing their life meant also having to face the same problems that rural people faced. These problems became accentuated towards the end of the sixties, with the failure of the Green Revolution. People were face to face with the development dilemma of the rich getting richer and the poor getting poorer and conflict situations were on the increase. The problems that rural people face are the problems of small farmers — or peasants, as we call them — who, once upon a time, had built vast irrigation reservoirs (called "tanks") and impressive temples, which nourished a great civilization. But today, the peasants of Sri Lanka, who are still the backbone of the nation, are fighting a desperate struggle for survival against the assaults of the prevailing neo-colonialist economic and social system with its multinationals, militarization, consumerism and accompanying cultural aggression.

The youth, especially, were most vocal about these problems and we came under heavy fire! They were intelligent enough to concede that they appreciated the Buddhist-Christian dialogue because it was something new and interesting and obviously necessary and of some value. But it was irrelevant to their most pressing needs! So Devasarana asked them to make the dialogue relevant, in other words, invited them to set the agenda! They said they wanted to study the problem of unemployment and discuss what should be done about it. Then, they themselves took a leading part in organizing a memorable one-and-a-half day seminar on unemployment in 1969. It began with readings from the Buddhist and Christian scriptures, a dialogue sermon in which a Buddhist bhikkhu and a Christian clergyman participated, and the eucharist. Stimulating talks and strenuous discussion followed, including discussion in small groups. The conclusion of the seminar was that land reform was necessary to solve unemployment.

Then an open People's Committee for Land Reform was set up in 1970 and a series of three seminars on land reform was held at Devasaranaramaya, the Ibbagamuwa Madhya Maha Vidyalaya and the Dehelgamuwa Temple. A book list on land reform was circulated and serious reading and study was done on the subject.

"Violent Lanka"

A fourth seminar was due to be held at Devasaranaramaya during the Sinhala-Tamil new year festival in April 1971 when the JVP-led insurrection broke out. It was crushed by the government of the time, with the help of several foreign countries. The Janatha Vimukti Peramuna was essentially a youth movement, immature and no doubt lacking in certain essential principles of correct political theory and action. But it is not enough to condemn it. The underlying causes of social unrest and the people affected by them must be sympathetically understood and concrete action taken to bring about the social changes necessary to solve the problems. "Violent Lanka," published by Devasarana at the time, attempted to point this out.

The time was unsettled but Devasarana pressed on with its tasks. The Devasarana collective farm was set up on St Barnabas' Day, 11 June 1971, on the Aramaya premises. Later, modifications had to be made in the collective farm set-up as the task of making collective structures work in a capitalist society was formidable. But, through many failures and some achievements, the experiment of the collective farm taught Devasarana lessons in the whole task of building true community life. A new way of life in common, new forms of production relationships and a new style of leadership needed to be evolved. Here, the collective principle had to be basic — not in order to stifle individual initiative but to enable it to be exercised for the common good.

Movement orientation

The collective farm was not an end in itself. It was a starting point for entering into the field of peasant organization. The peasant movement has been a major concern. Devasarana has initiated or helped a number of projects such as farms, credit societies, small industries, medical clinics, pre-schools, etc. But, essentially, Devasarana has been movement-oriented and not project-oriented. It recognizes the existence of a development-justice-liberation movement in the historical situation and attempts to participate in it. The Buddhist-Christian-Marxist dialogue evolved out of that participation. That point needs to be emphasized. The dialogue was not thought out or planned in armchairs. It is not an abstract academic exercise. It arose out of participation in the struggle of the people for justice. Thus it is a living dialogue of people of various faiths and ideologies involved in a common struggle. Here it is necessary to distinguish between "syncretism" and "integration". "Syncretism"[2] is a mixture of various elements which tend to remain apart, conflict or pull in different directions, resulting in domination, disharmony and confusion. Integration is the interaction of diverse traditions or identities in harmony, where the different traditions enrich each other without losing their identity. There is a growth towards unity in diversity, which produces creative action. This is part of the "new ecumenism" or "wider ecumenism" that the church throughout the world is discovering in this present era, in living and working together with people of other religions and ideologies.

New world liturgy

In the common struggle serious difficulties and obstacles have to be faced: the disillusionment with traditional forms of worship which are incapable of nourishing and sustaining those in the forefront of peoples' struggles, a recurring sense of futility and the tendency towards disunity in the face of the powerful assaults of the powers-that-be, having to persevere in pursuance of goals despite repeated failure. To meet these challenges there was the need to rally, renew and pool all available resources of mind and spirit. In this process, through much agony as well as much solidarity and joy, was evolved the new world liturgy (translation of the Sinhala term "Nava Lo Vandana"). It is a liturgy drawn from the resources of the major religions and ideologies, on the common theme of development-justice-liberation, in which all committed people may join to celebrate.

Church tradition

Bishop Lakshman Wickremesinghe was a guide, counsellor and friend through all these searchings and adventurings. He succeeded Bishop De Mel as Bishop of Kurunegala and Upadhyaya of Devasaranaramaya in 1962. During an episcopate of twenty-one years he grew, through a creative response to social realities, into a radical, living expression of dharma in its wider and deeper reaches. It may also be said that part of this exploration was done in partnership with Devasarana. There was much opposition from certain sections of the church to the work of Devasarana, and Bishop Lakshman had the delicate task of mediation! He did not always agree with Devasarana but he recognized the right of the Aramaya to freedom for responsible criticism and experiment. There was a creative tension and Bishop Lakshman always remained in dialogue to encourage as well as restrain, to guide as well as advise and warn. He was an important link between the Aramaya and church tradition at its best.

While criticizing arrogance and domination, corruption, hypocrisy and irrelevance in the church, Devasarana had always sought to do so in the spirit of "speaking the truth in love", though, no doubt, not always succeeding! At the same time, it has been conscious of its own weaknesses and shortcomings and has always looked to the true tradition of the church for inspiration and solidarity.

Encounter with the people

But, fundamentally, it was the encounter with the masses of the people and their leaders and organizations at grassroots level, situated in their culture and engaged in their struggles, arising out of their daily problems, for a better, more human way of life, that has made Devasarana what it is. The impact of many veteran peasant leaders can never be forgotten. The distilled wisdom of their long experience and their tenacity of purpose and unremitting persistence in the progressive movement, alongside the people, in the face of continuing obstacles, were truly remarkable. Then there were the emerging young leaders, who also made a powerful impact. The urgency of their thirst for change, their simple and rigorous life-style, their insistence on the discipline of self-criticism and mutual criticism, their openness to new approaches and their readiness to learn from the people have enabled them to mature through the trials and sufferings of the struggle for justice.

Then, there were the bhikkhus in the broad progressive movement, both the older and younger people. They took their stand alongside the people, making dharma relevant to actual social realities, leading Satyagraha or at the head of the picket line but, above all, by just being themselves, a living embodiment of the culture of the people. Devasarana learnt much from them too.

Finally, there were the women with their dual concern for women's rights and participation in peoples' struggles for social change. Their association with Devasarana has made a tremendous difference to the attitudes and perspectives of Devasarana. The style of leadership, language, jokes of the men, all came under judgment! This has had a stimulating effect in liberating human relationships, though not without some tension and pain. Here the process of learning has only started. There is a long way still to go!

Two other related spheres in the peoples' movement must be mentioned, namely, the ethnic conflict and the whole subject of civil, democratic and human rights. With the steady deterioration of the economic and social situation in the country, the ethnic conflict as well as the whole subject of civil, democratic and human rights reached critical and tragic proportions. These were intimately bound up with the total situation of the country as a whole and so seriously affected every sphere of the nation's life — peasants, workers, students, and religious and social organization in general. So Devasarana was drawn towards involvement in these spheres.

Workers and peasants struggles

There have been many significant movements, occasions or campaigns in the people's movement and some instances of these are worth recording here. A crucial moment was the general strike of 1980, when large numbers of striking workers were "locked out" and thus lost their jobs. The Organization for Obtaining Justice for Strikers was set up. Solidarity committees were set up in different parts of the country and meetings, satyagrahas, protests and demonstrations were held to get back the jobs of the workers. Then the government policy of large-scale take-over of land used by peasants, consequent on the extension of the operation of multinationals to the peasant sector, resulted in the organization of a mammoth peasant petition, with village-to-village and house-to-house visiting and meetings in several districts of the country. This included a major peasant demonstration in Colombo in September 1982. The ongoing peasant struggle in Moneragala against the sugar multinationals is a continuation of it. Then, again, the Pavidi Handa (voice of clergy) movement of Buddhist and Christian clergy against the suppression of democratic rights during the Referendum of 1982 and the famous Pavidi Handa human rights case in the supreme court resulting in a historic verdict was another instance. The Campaign for Release of Political Prisoners (CROPP), launched towards the end of 1985, and the agitation against the water tax are other instances. These and other such movements or occasions were rallying-points of the people's movement. Despite the limited success, in the short term, of particular campaigns, the people grew through these in gaining understanding of their situation and in organizing themselves for change.

Changes

With the involvement of Devasarana in these various concerns, there were certain changes in the life and organization of Devasarana. In the beginning, the pattern of life and work was monastic, with its regular times, forms and practices, even though the intention of "new creation" had been there from the beginning. Then, while being faithful to the original vision and principles, a new rhythm of life and work was explored where there was more freedom and flexibility to respond to the actual condition of society, particularly to the challenge of the poor and the need to make the option for the poor. With increasing involvements there were increasing difficulties and problems. The spiritual dimension was ever more necessary. But new and deeper spiritual resources had to be found. This meant a continuing search for and continuing discovery — a continuing formation, with all the failures and frustrations involved — of "a spirituality for our times".

This change of emphasis resulted in certain organizational changes too. The membership of Devasaranaramaya was opened to both men and women, married as well as single, and there was the working out of new disciplines suited for the new context. So, there are now families resident at Devasarana, as well as single people of both sexes. Further, the Devasarana Development Centre (DDC) has been set up on the same premises to organize the development work.

The emergence of collective leadership from the masses has been the most encouraging feature of the Devasarana history. The original leadership, as described earlier, had been predominantly upper-class and elite. It had its advantages and disadvantages. It had a certain historic function to perform. But the disastrous consequences of perpetuating such leadership in a changing society were clearly evident in society at large. Leadership has become basically out of touch with the needs of the masses. So the fundamental aim at Devasarana was to facilitate the emergence of the leadership of the future that would arise from the struggle of the working classes. In this, professionals, intellectuals, etc. from other classes would be allies, but would not dominate.

There is wealth of talent and skills among the masses. There is also an emerging leadership involved in the struggle of the masses and in living touch with the masses. But this emerging leadership is without power and without opportunity to effectively serve the masses. Devasarana seeks to facilitate the emergence of this leadership.

Linkage

Devasarana's links with the world community must also be referred to here. It is essential to be based firmly on indigenous resources, values and leadership. There must also be independence in policy and decision-making. But, at the same time, the importance of the principle of linkage and solidarity has to be recognized. Just as linkage and solidarity within a country are important, so are linkage and solidarity at regional and world levels. For Devasarana, this has come mainly through the Asian Regional

Fellowship (ARF) and the Commission on the Churches' Participation in Development (CCPD) of the World Council of Churches. The ARF is an association of development groups in India, Sri Lanka, Thailand, Philippines, Indonesia and South Korea. Also related to ARF are the Asian Cultural Forum on Development (ACFOD), which is an association of representatives from eighteen countries, and the Economic and Social Commission for Asia and the Pacific (ESCAP), both UN-related bodies. In CCPD there are links between development groups in Latin America, USA, Europe and African countries, in addition to the Asian countries already mentioned.

There is sharing of resources and sharing of experience through programmes of mutual visiting, mutual help, conferences, seminars, common study, research and training programmes, etc. In this matter of sharing of resources, material resources, finance and technology are important, but far more important are human and spiritual resources — religion and culture, experience, understanding and vision, experience of oppression, preservation of the will to resist, understanding of the need for change and of the processes of change, endurance and perseverance in the struggle, comradeship and solidarity. These are the basic ingredients of the emerging new humanity and new society. Also, most important, there has to be true partnership. Whether between East and West, North and South, black and white, rich and poor, men and women, there has to be giving and receiving, learning and teaching on both sides.

Violence and ahimsa

A word must be said about violence, thought it is too large a subject to be gone into fully here. Sri Lanka, like so many countries in the world, has been plagued with it. Devasarana and many other allied organizations have agonized over the issues involved. Violence has always been "a concomitant" of social change. There are certain realities involved in it that have to be recognized. But that does not mean that one should be reconciled to violence. Ahimsa will always be an innermost yearning of the heart. So there has to be a fundamental commitment to ahimsa, non-violence. But not a passive non-violence. Bishop Lakshman Wickremesinghe used to challenge Devasarana to search for a dynamic non-violence that actively opposes injustice and yields nothing to the oppressor, but does not break the bonds of love. That search must go on through sacrifice, crisis and challenge and vicarious suffering. It is a process of perfecting maithriya, agape, love. It is a fundamental commitment in the building of the new humanity. If the struggle ends in "victory" without understanding what it means to be truly human, that is, without giving rise to a more humane way of life for all people, it would all have been in vain.

Spirituality for our times

So the living dialogue must go on. Here the theistic religions — Hinduism, Christianity and Islam — and the philosophies of Buddhism, secular humanism and Marxism, can be united in the search for "a spirituality for our times". The dialogue has to be rooted in ancient verities but free and flexible to respond to new and creative forces arising out of changing conditions. There are, no doubt, negative and corrupting aspects of materialism and secularism. But there are healthy and vital aspects of the whole secularization process. This process will never be reversed, as far as one could visualize. In the common search for a new spirituality with Buddhists, secular humanists and Marxists, theists must be prepared to shed, or at least be detached enough to reinterpret, certain transcendental theological forms and concepts which are not of the essence of dharma or doctrine. But, always, there must be unrelenting search for the truth — not only "beyond-the-beyond" but "beyond in the midst" — "ever further beyond and ever deeper within"! And always, it must be through "praxis", action-reflection and living dialogue.

NOTES

[1] Srama, from which the word shramadana comes, really means essential activity and asrama means intense essential activity. Ram means divine or essential joy and aram means intense joy. Aramas were originally gardens which were gifted to the Sangha as places for rest and refreshment.

[2] Some theologians have tried to rehabilitate the term "syncretism" in the creative sense of integration. But it is more commonly used in the sense given here.

Experience of Spirituality in Dialogue

JOHN C. ENGLAND

John England, who had also spent a considerable part of his life in Asia, affirmed the close relation between personal spiritual life and the commitment to the struggles in the world. His own experience with the Satyodaya community in Sri Lanka demonstrated for him the "natural blessing of friendship and work, of struggle and reflection where personal life and life of the group embodied some of the simplicities of hope, compassion and justice".

Two pictures have long focused for me the reality of spirituality in dialogue (although each is only one of any that could be chosen from early Christian communities in Asia and the contemporary networks of centres and movements in the region).

One picture is of a village, Sheuiyan, flourishing 1000 years ago in Turkestan near Balayik, Turfan. As in numerous other places on many old silk roads and sea trade-routes, Buddhists and also Christians had established hospices, monasteries, churches and communities. We know from the manuscripts discovered in the ruined church of Sheuiyan that it was in use for almost 900 years, and this is not unusual. But what is most notable for us is that these early Asian (Nestorian) Christians show us a long history both of service in medical care, education, state service and trade, and *also* of friendly co-existence and mutual borrowing with Buddhists, Manichees and Muslims. It lasted until the Crusades.

The other picture is of a small interfaith community, Satyodaya, in Kandy, Sri Lanka — where for 12 years the team, drawn from each of Lanka's religious traditions, has undertaken adult education, village welfare, inter-racial reconciliation and refugee work. Self-support, social research, and theological reflection (especially in the writing of Paul

Caspersz) has also been central. At considerable risk, amidst recent disturbances, Satyodaya and sister centres have fostered awareness, worked for a human community, and shared the spirit of hope and justice. These two pictures, taken from many, sum up the dimensions of spirituality which have meant most to me.

If I was to mention my own story of a growing experience of spirituality in dialogue, I would have to describe the discovery of ecumenical fellowship in church life, social concern and theological reflection, which came first through the Student Christian Movement; years on the staff of the East Asia Christian Conference (later CCA) which threw me into the "secular" and "spiritual" engagement of Christians and others throughout the region (in the related tasks of people's education, lay-training, community action and theological reflection); and the growing use, in devotional life and daily life-style, of resources from many spiritualities (of meditation and struggle).

But I would prefer to talk more of certain directions of spirituality which are to me fundamental in our concern. Where is this search and pilgrimage in spirituality leading us? What moves us on?

In my own case, it was certainly by responding to what was experienced as a call within one Christian tradition that I have been led further and further into an ever wider ecumenism. It was not a decision to seek a "religious experience" as such; not my major endeavour to enter into the insights and experience of another religious tradition. But this has become increasingly important to me once I was caught up in the life-style and spirituality of those with whom I was working: in mass education, student groups, lay-centres and movements for social concern or theological reflection, with many friends in different countries — whether Muslim community workers in Malaysia and Indonesia; Buddhist monks and lay people in Sri Lanka or Thailand; Sarvodaya workers in India; or Marxist teachers in the Philippines; to mention only a few. The process has been, in an important sense, more worldly than religious: a "dialogue of life".

Here was a different spirituality, which arose in the midst of daily life: a "natural" blending of friendship and work, of struggle and reflection where personal life and life of the group embodied some of the simplicities of hope, compassion and justice. And in work together for a shared goal, we "found each other together on the road to God's new world" (perhaps the best description of *any* ecumenical/interfaith endeavour!). Because of friendship, solidarity, co-existence and mutual acceptance in a commitment to work for creative and just communities, we were led to a deeper affirmation of what humanity is, and what from each of the traditions sustains specifically human values. We were led from questions as to "how to survive", humanly and Christianly, to celebrating the reign of God's love and justice; and beyond any dualism of the "spiritual" and the "worldly" to find the unity of personal transformation and social transformation without which any spirituality can only be partial.

From these endeavours and affirmations, in which many, many of our colleagues are now sharing, flows a stream of reflection and insight, a rich literature of contemporary theology which it has been my privilege also to assist in collecting and sharing (now within the Programme for Theology and Cultures in Asia).

But if we are to share our own experiences of spirituality in dialogue (and, I must add, in life and struggle) with others, especially in our churches, and foster a larger view and experience of the one living God which we learn with our neighbours, I suggest we must begin with a few simple questions. Not only "how can we unite the searches for personal and for social transformation?" and "how do we find each other on the road to these?" but also:

a) "Where do we think the church is?" Is it not as fully and genuinely present already in our centres and movements, our basic Christian communities, lay ministries, as in any local "church"?

b) Where is the discovery of openness, larger truth, of "each other on the road" happening already, and what has helped it to happen?

c) What are the resources — personal, in writing, in communities — available, and being used, for this?

Deepening our Understanding of Spirituality

YVES RAGUIN, SJ

"Many Christians object to the use of a mantra of prayer," says Yves Raguin, director of the Ricci Institute for Chinese Studies in Taipei, "simply because mantra is used in Transcendental Meditation. They say that the mantra used has some religious connotation that is not Christian, but Hindu." Coming out of a long experience of Buddhist meditation, Raguin argues that mantra is a method and has no religious meaning. The practice of ways of concentration and awareness taken from other traditions helped him in the development of a Christian spiritual discipline.

The aim of this paper is to explain how we can use non-Christian ways of prayer and meditation to aid us in fostering our Christian spiritual experience. What I say is based on my own experience and on the experience of many other people I have been working with for many years, especially after I arrived in China in 1949 and later lived in Vietnam and in Taiwan. This experience is not based on dialogue with Buddhist monks or Taoist devotees, but on what I call inner dialogue within myself. I studied some Hinduism, but my field has been mostly Chinese Buddhism, Taoism and Confucianism. This is the reason why I know Buddhist and Taoist spirituality better than any other spiritualities. By practising ways of inner concentration and awareness taken from these traditions, I have better understood Christian spirituality. This helped me to rediscover aspects of Christian spirituality which had been neglected during the past centuries. From this way of inner dialogue, using such methods, I came to a deeper understanding of the mystery of life in Christ.

A few years ago, I was asked to give a lecture at the University of Santo Tomas in Manila, on the topic St Teresa of Avila and Oriental mysticism. At first I did not know how to react, but very quickly I realized that Teresa's mystical experience was related to a "three-level" structure of a human being: body, soul and spirit. She was familiar with the division: body and soul, but to explain her mystical experience of God dwelling in her, she had to say: "Of course the soul is one, but the centre of the soul is so different that we have to call it 'spirit', because this is the place where God who is spirit has his dwelling place."

From Teresa I went back to the Chinese philosophers and spiritual men and I realized that in the three Chinese traditions, Confucianism, Taoism and Buddhism, the structure of human beings was always a "three-level" one. In the three traditions, body and heart are named the same way but the third and deeper level has different names. This third level is the one through which we reach the world beyond. In Confucianism this third level is called human nature, in Taoism it is called primordial breath or spirit, in Buddhism it is called original nature. According to the Confucian philosopher Mencius, "if I exert all the capacities of my heart, I know my human nature. To know one's nature is to know heaven."[1] This sentence spoke to me. To know what it is to be a human being leads us to the knowledge of heaven and God, since our human nature is the gift of heaven. In Taoism the same principle applies. The primordial breath animates everything. In the human person it is identical to the spirit. At the level of the spirit a person can arrive at oneness with the Tao. In Buddhism one's original nature is identical to the Buddha nature which is the absolute ground of everything.

At the same time, I realized that the yoga methods were built on a similar "three-level" structure: body, heart and spirit or self. From these Oriental traditions I turned back to our Christian anthropology. I realized immediately that St Paul's spiritual experience was expressed within a similar structure. He writes to the Thessalonians: "May the God of peace make you perfect and holy; and may you all be kept safe and blameless, spirit, soul and body, for the coming of our Lord Jesus Christ" (1 Thess. 5:23). Studying Paul's letters, I realized that this structure was to be found everywhere in his writings.

The most important point for spiritual life is the distinction between soul and spirit or "heart" and spirit. If we do not make a distinction between the two it is impossible to explain what we call the spiritual life. The spirit is the centre of the soul or heart, and the deepest part of it. It is one with the soul and, at the same time, very different from it. That distinction, which is difficult to make if we rely on psychological experience, becomes clear if we see it from the point of view of God. This is the reason why we find in the letter to the Hebrews this text which is so important for our topic: "The word of God is something alive and active: it cuts like any double-edged sword but more finely: it can clip through the place where the soul is divided from the spirit" (Heb. 4:12). This distinction is found in the Gospels also.

The Zen experience is based on a few very simple principles, which are quite well-known.

1. The way to the ultimate experience of oneness with the absolute reality is not based on a relationship to God through a mediator. The way to this ultimate experience is through the realization of the oneness of a person's original nature with the Buddha nature and with the absolute reality.

2. At the depth of our human being lies our "original nature" which is absolutely pure. If the Zen monk sits in "Zen" meditation, it is because he believes in the presence in himself of this human nature.

3. Such being our original nature, it is beyond our grasp. We cannot reach it, understand it, describe it. We can only wait for it to manifest itself and shine at the depth of our human being. This manifestation which will be a real enlightenment is beyond our power, because our original nature is in fact Buddha nature.

4. To arrive at the enlightenment, the best we can do is to sit in pure attentiveness to our original nature. We cannot think about it, and even less imagine it. This is the reason why the great masters of Zen tell us of the principles of the method: no thinking, no relying on, no attachment. This creates a real "emptying" of the "heart", which becomes void. This does not mean that the Zen contemplative faces "nothing". He faces his own original nature through void and emptiness.

From Zen practice I learned not to search for a God on high, a transcendent God, but I turned towards my inner being, facing my human nature. Since my human nature is God's image, I simply wait for this God's image to manifest itself to me. I learned from Christ to be simply attentive to my inner mystery, knowing that I cannot see my face as God's child, unless the Father enlightens me by his own Spirit.

The practice of Zen meditation taught me to stay in pure attentiveness before my inner mystery. No thinking could make me realize this inner mystery of mine. I could not rely on any thought, any desire, to reach this presence of God in me. When I was told not to think, not to rely on anything, I was a little disturbed. I was not allowed to think of Christ. Then I realized, after some years, that the last step of the gospel is not to follow Christ or to imitate him. These are necessary steps, but the last step of the gospel is taken when Christ says: "It is good for you that I go." We could comment: "You will not see me any more before you, you will not be able to rely on my external presence, but I will be in you."[2]

In fact it is the practice of Zen which helped me to understand that the final step is not to follow Christ or to imitate him, but to be animated by him, because he lives in us. I realized at the same time that in *The Cloud of Unknowing* Christ is no more an object of contemplation, but the one who living in us, stirs in us this intent of love which turns our attention towards God himself, the God who cannot be known by knowing, but only by unknowing.

I realized at the same time that the way of prayer of Jesus when he was alone was more of the Zen type. He was simply aware that all his life was sharing the life of the Father. He was not meditating but simply aware that, at the depth of his human nature, he shared divine nature with his Father. This is why I dare to say that the practice of Zen led me to a deeper understanding of God's presence in me and of Christ's way of prayer.

Fullness and emptiness in spiritual life

In Taoist tradition life is very important. The inner energy coming from the Tao through the primordial breath circulates in our body and animates every part of it. The Taoist adept will "sit in forgetting". This means that the first step will be to forget all the external things in order to focus on the inner experience. By centring on the inner experience, the meditator "nourishes" one's inner life, one's inner nature and one's spirit. While nourishing this inner energy and making it circulate in every part of his body, one feels a fullness of life. Slowly breathing makes us aware of this inner life circulating. As the experience deepens, one becomes aware of the source of life, the Tao itself.

While practising this way of contemplation, I became aware of the importance of life in John's Gospel. From the beginning, John tells us that the word of God is the life of everything. Everything in the universe has life in this word of God. Later on the theme of life associated with the spirit symbolized by water occurs several times in John's Gospel, for example when Jesus talks with Nicodemus and with the Samaritan woman. Many times the Lord speaks of eternal life, which is not the life we will receive after death, but the deepest level of our life in Christ.

From the awareness of the fullness of physical life in me, I opened myself to a deeper life, the life of the heart, which is psychological, and the life at the level of the spirit which is spiritual life flowing from God.

This is what I call the "way of fullness". It is the easiest way of contemplation. It makes us feel in deep harmony with oneself, and also with the whole of creation. We feel really that we are part of a universe inhabited by God and full of God's presence and energy.

But following the Taoist masters as well as the Buddhist ones, I realized that I could be so full of peace and joy that I could be seduced by them. Now I realize that this fullness of the heart can be an obstacle to my union with God. Here the mystics in every tradition, Taoist or Buddhist, reminded me that I had to empty my heart in order to reach the level of the spirit where God dwells. Finding this "fasting of the heart" in Taoist tradition,[3] the "emptying of the heart" in Buddhism, I was brought back to our mystical tradition of the "night of the soul" of St John of the Cross. Finally I saw the teaching of Christ on "losing one's life" in order to have eternal life, on dying in order to live, in a new perspective.

Again and again, I listened to the mystics of other religions and they made me understand better the meaning of death to oneself in Christian life. We have to make our "heart" die if we want the spirit to be alive in us. Looking at the death of Christ in these perspectives I understood that during his passion he went through the absolute emptying of his physical and psychological life. But through this death he realized that at the level of the spirit he was fully alive. This is the reason why, just before dying, he said: "Father, into your hands I commit my spirit" (Luke 23:46).

I may say that it is under the influence of these Taoist and Buddhist ways of emptiness that I entered into a deeper understanding of Christ's way of emptiness and death.

Many people object to these kinds of practices. They tell us that Zen method cannot be separated from Buddhism, and that Taoist ways of contemplation cannot be Christanized. They forget that Christianity never had any method of its own, because Christ never taught any method. On the contrary John the Baptist did teach ways of prayer. When Christ was asked: "Master, teach us how to pray", he did not teach a method. He presented the content of our prayers. He never told his disciples to sit, or to stand, or to meditate, or to contemplate... The first Christians followed the Jewish ways of prayer.

Methods belong to the level of body and heart. I elaborate them the way I want. They are common to everybody. I may sit exactly like a Buddhist monk, I may breathe like him. But the difference will be in what we believe. My Buddhist friend sits, empties his heart, because he wants to reach Buddhist enlightenment. As a Christian, I sit and breathe the way he does, but I want to have a Christian enlightenment. Here is the difference, not in the psychological method but in the aim presented by faith. The enlightenment does not depend on myself. It is a grace coming from God. For my Buddhist friend, enlightenment is not the fruit of his efforts. It is a gift from his deep nature which is the transcendent Buddha nature.

Many Christians object to the use of a mantra for prayer, simply because mantra is used in Transcendental Meditation. They say that the mantra used has some religious connotation, not Christian, but Hindu. The mantra is a method. If I choose the name of Jesus as a mantra, I use the method of repetition in a Christian perspective. We know from history that most of the practices used by monks and ascetics during the first centuries of Christianity were borrowed from other religions. And we know that some of these traditions originated in India. This seems to be the case of the so-called "Jesus prayer" which appeared among Egyptian hermits rather early in history. This method of repetition is very conducive to an inner experience of Christ's presence in us.

Dialogue at the level of spirituality is fundamental. Theological reflection can easily remain at the intellectual level. Spiritual experience has to be lived in daily life. It cannot remain on the theoretical level. This is why it is so important to see how ways of spiritual life in other religions can be used by Christians. The ultimate result will be a deeper and wider understanding of the Christian faith. Christ's stature will not be lowered. On the contrary he will be more easily recognized as the Son of God.

NOTES

[1] *The Four Books of Mencius,* Book VII, Chapter 2, Section 1.
[2] Y. Raguin, "Christianity and Zen", *East Asian Pastoral Review,* Vol. XX, 1983, No. 4, pp.345-350.
[3] The expression "fasting of the heart" comes from Chuang-tzu, Book IV, the world of man.

From Diverse Situations

The following four reflections indicate the vastly different situations in which Christians and churches find themselves in relating to neighbours of other faiths.

Brother Khalil Zomkhol from the Orthodox St George's Monastery in Lebanon speaks about the "wonderful, silent, spiritual dialogue established at the centre between Christian monasticism in the Orient and Islam". Hakan Eilert, a Lutheran from Sweden, shares his theological struggles as he faced the challenge of using Buddhist disciplines to enhance his own understanding of Christian life and discipline and suggests that his own convictions about Christ were confirmed in this spiritual encounter. Arnold Bittlinger, who is primarily engaged in research on charismatic renewal, using the disciplines of depth psychology, shows how he sees the inter-relation between a number of dimensions of life in the spirit. Colin Alcock shares his experience of taking the first steps in Australia to relate the traditional Christian spirituality to aboriginal spirituality.

Oneness at the Centre

KHALIL ZOMKHOL

The spiritual path — particularly in its Christian form — is fundamentally a quest for the Spirit. It therefore has the appearance of a quest for the "Rising Sun that never sets" — a spiritual Orient — or the "Sun of

Righteousness". It is, we may say, a "circular path". Consequently it is dialogue with the Wholly Other in the unity of the Centre. It is the Way of Hospitality — *philoxenia,* love of the stranger.

Because we have forgotten this we have for centuries been "set" and bogged down in the "linear path" of our Western world of sunset or decline, our interior "occident", which as a "path" lacks direction — in it we are dis*orient*ed, turned away from the Rising Sun, "de-centred" and without hospitality. (The discoveries of a "new world" were to set the seal on this. There the "work of human hands" — technical progress — turning away from its true purpose — tried to "displace" God, and so to enslave humanity more effectively.) On this linear, one-dimensional, external path, unhappily, treasures of faith and zeal became trivialized and every "spiritual work" of "love", heroic though it might be, now appears as a factor not of liberation but of alienation. Today the Spirit seems to be saying to us, "I have this against you, that you have forgotten your first love", your own centre.

The wonderful, silent spiritual dialogue established at the centre between Christian monasticism in the Orient and Islam therefore appears like a splendid witness to that "circular path" with its orientation towards the centre. Of this path it reminds us through the memory of the Spirit which Jesus of Nazareth left us as his will and testament and which comes up from within. As first and last love.

The *Centre* is the Royal Road of — and towards — the Holy Spirit of dialogue, in which, as it were, this Spirit dwells, as in an ecumenical "interior castle" or temple. There we discover the Spirit of Jesus Christ is present already, with all humanity, and this happens in so far as we make room for people and offer them hospitality. "Behold I stand at the door and *wait...*" The Son of Man, wholly of the past but, since Pentecost, poured out in the Spirit, appears after his resurrection as the "only stranger[1] in Jerusalem" (Luke 24). In Greek hospitality means "love of the stranger" *(philoxenia)*. "Stranger" in Arabic is *gharib* and has the sense of "someone who goes on pilgrimage to the far west", the interior "occident" (where the sun goes down or declines — for it is the place of decline), seeking the "Rising Sun" (the Orient) "which cannot set" and which is the Centre where the Spirit of God dwells. Everyone is a "stranger" and even an "enemy", depending on how far I am "institutionalized" or "set" in my path to this interior west, this "occident" of the declining sun. In this way, then, all human beings, strangers or enemies, carry within them my salvation. "But I say unto you, love your enemies." I discover that I am the stranger's "neighbour", the stranger's brother, as I "approach" him or her, wounded as they are, with mercy, the balm from the womb of the Spirit, for "the Spirit is the Mother". All of a sudden the stranger reveals the Spirit to me — is the Spirit's challenge — and has mysteriously led me towards him. Human beings are Spirit, transparent, icon-like. If the word reveals the Father and the Spirit reveals the Lordship of Jesus, human beings reveal the Spirit. Human beings are icons — images *(eikones)* — of the Spirit. The Spirit is the communion (koinonia) of human beings, of each human being. He lays us bare at the centre.

Each person, like a mirror, throws back the neighbour to his or her own centre. Merely by being and becoming "themselves", in their own centre, everyone has a mission to drag others back from forgetfulness of their own centre. Already that is dialogue. In Arabic "dialogue" suggests revolving round an axis. Any centrifugal path rises in a spiral. This dialogue in the utmost otherness establishes itself naturally, as if spontaneously, because the centre, the dwelling-place of the Spirit of God is also the "where that is no-where" of the Spirit of the divine word. This is the prime dialogue within the Godhead which discloses to humans their fundamental *responsibility*. This responsibility is on the plane of being and of nature by the very fact that individuals recognize they are interrogated by God and at the same time interrogate him: "He who answers and He who questions", as Ibn Arabi the Sufi subtly put it, "is God himself".

Thus the dialogue is spontaneously created from one centre of responsibility to the other. In communion. And there is but one centre.

Islam, which is centred to a high degree, represents a call and a reminder to the divided, disoriented church to attach itself again to its own centre. Meanwhile, there is a deep mutual sympathy between Islam and monasticism, expressed in instances of friendship and cooperation. Islamic history likes to trace this back to its beginnings. The secret of this deep mutual attraction has perhaps not been adequately understood. It is all the more fundamental and full of promise since at its starting-point it signals that its source is in what is yet to come. With a backcloth of transparency common to the two different faiths: the sacrificial hospitality of their common father, Abraham. The secret here is simply the centre around which all people in their own way collect themselves in meditation and unfold.

"Am I not your Lord?" In Islam all gather together in prayer in *concentric circles* around this primal divine interrogative, symbolized by the Black Stone (Kaaba, Arabic *ka'bah*), as if around their *centre*. There are nearly two million of them at Mecca at the festival of (Abraham's) sacrifice (of a sheep), from all races and "confessions" and tendencies, forgetting their differences, divergences or conflicts to proclaim and repeat together their witness of faith in the oneness or unity *(tawhid),* Lordship and Mercy of God.

"Father, may they be one as You and I are one, so that the world may believe that You have sent me." Strangely — be it said to our shame — it is Islam, not Christendom, which will be keeping the appointment. The wind (the Spirit) blows where it wills. Islam, the "poor relation" *outside* the church, joins the monk who is the "poor relation" *inside.* "The monk is at the heart of the mystery of the unity of the church", at the centre. But the circle is an extension from the centre. Circle and centre are one.

Now, here we have the "monastic" icon (eikon, image) of the centre, of the One — of peace. It is displayed by the Eastern church for the veneration of the faithful at the feast of Pentecost. The mutual, infinite love between the Father and the Son is the Holy Spirit "in person". This unity of love is what the icon painted by André Roublev the monk tries to outline by means of the circumference-less circle of three angels who seem to interpenetrate each other. In the centre is communion; the communication to humanity of this divine life in the form of a sacrificial eucharistic cup, with the Sacrificial Lamb. Thus, shining through Abraham's hospitality offered to three Strangers, the wholly primordial "divine council" — willing the *theosis* (or divinization) of humanity — is delineated, central in ecclesial communion. This we owe to the silent response of the Son of Man, the archetypal Elder Brother of the first Adam — who comes, too, proleptically, to bring him out of his confused distress with God's first *interrogative:* "Adam, where art thou?" The Son is there, at the very same time, in the bosom of the Father, on the cross and in humanity. And when he has gone, his Spirit, like a murmuring stream, takes up that *question* again as a clear-cut call: "Come to the Father." And, in oneness with the human spirit, He will call "Abba, Father" — with the meaningful reality shining through.

Be it noted that in this icon of the centre we can also easily see the organic unity which in Oriental lands makes the various streams in the revelation come together: spirituality, scripture, theology (the life within the Godhead), the economy of salvation, liturgy, ecclesiology and anthropology.

The Christian monk and the Islamic sufi, each thus centred in his own faith, display coherence in their internal logic as they embark on the long, difficult, adventurous pilgrimage towards that interior Orient, the centre of which is the heart transfigured into the dwelling-place of peace, rest, and the unity of beauty (Hesychasm). This is where the flame of the memory (Arabic: *zikr*) of God, coming up from within, is kept alight in his holy Name, as if by some "tongue of fire".

Monk — cf. *mon*(ach)*os* in Greek — means "one", someone who loves the One, a seeker of the kingdom of God alone and of his justice. "Find peace within" is the advice of Seraphim of Sarov to a disciple, "and thousands around you will find salvation."

"Preaching", in Arabic, and "centre" go back to the same source. Because Mary, at the Master's feet, was centred on the One Thing Needful, the Gospel is preached throughout the world.

NOTE

[1] Cf. Greek *paroikeis,* Latin *peregrinus* in the context, the latter meaning a sojourner away from home and so ultimately a pilgrim.

Journey through the Gateless Gate

HAKAN EILERT

The world was changing, and fast. After the second world war the distance between various parts of the globe was eliminated. Different cultures were no longer inaccessible. We lived in each other's backyards. We lived in a global village.

European culture and religion could no longer be regarded as the supreme expressions of the human spirit. Western colonialism was gradually dismantled and when television sets were installed in our homes, we watched the emerging nations in Africa and Asia sometimes rejecting the values they had been asked to accept. On the map, Europe looked like a beak-shaped protrusion on the body of Asia. A political and economic restructuring was set in motion. Mercator's world map became outdated.

Perplexed Westerners found that other world religions were still very much alive. Indian swamis toured Europe. Transcendental Meditation, Zen and scientology made inroads in Paris, Stockholm and Zürich. Young Europeans dressed in yellow robes danced to the glory of Krishna in Piccadilly Circus. Turbans appeared in the subway.

It was a time of insecurity. Had we not been taught that religion belonged to the past? Had we not been told that the death of Christianity was apparent and that the churches and religious institutions served as storehouses for the perennial harvest of human unhappiness?

Christian theology was on the retreat. The signals from the East were usually ignored. Faculties in Europe were mainly occupied with internal issues like the process of democracy, women's liberation, equality, etc.

Among students of theology, however, there was a search. I was one of them. Some of us found that while *theologia propria* failed to communicate the spiritual dimension this task was undertaken by other disciplines. We discovered C.G. Jung and Erich Fromm and became aware of the life of the spirit expressing itself in the language of the human psyche. Martin Buber, T.S. Eliot and Thomas Merton were avidly read. Some of us discussed Dostoyevsky. A widening of the horizon was desperately needed and we struggled like drowning people.

We didn't, however, know how to handle our search. There were no teachers to guide us, but somehow we sensed that a dialogical approach would be in order. The life of faith had nothing to do with the isolation of a Robinson Crusoe. There were footsteps in the sand: someone to discover — my fellow man or woman, my neighbour. Religion was not a solitary voyage, a heroic thrust to grasp heavenly life for my own benefit, neither was it a passive listening in the pews of the local churches. Martin Luther King Jr, Malcolm X and Che, Mao-tse Tung and Luthuli, US bombing Vietnam on Christmas Eve: what was happening in the world? It became clear that the subject of theology was just these facets of human life.

Young people all over the world reacted almost in unison — planting flowers in rifle barrels, holding hands, demanding change, freedom and human dignity for the oppressed. Church and mission were severely criticized. It was no longer credible to talk about God in an objectifying manner. God was involved in the suffering of people who were denied or deprived basic human rights.

Even the idea of truth was questioned. Orthodoxy in isolation became a non-issue. No truth could live its own independent life. Truth needed to relate to my neighbour's presence here and now. Without "you" there is no "I". Action and outreach became the criterion of Christian life.

I moved to Japan and my questioning took a new turn. The plurality of religions became a problem. What about the absoluteness of Christ? Jews, Muslims and Buddhists expressed their religious convictions in different ways. But instead of retreating into a dogmatic cocoon I somehow dimly perceived that humankind's religious and cultural diversity was not to be deplored. Were not the religious traditions an asset to be appreciated and affirmed in their richness and variety? Symbols and myths opened up deeper layers of meaning (Eliade, Tillich) and I found that the biblical testimony came alive in a new and richer key. I found that God was not primarily interested in Christianity but in humanity.

So it became necessary to get to know other traditions dispensing with the well-meaning guidance of Western text-books. A fascinating exploration started. It became clear that the institutional church needed to break through its own provincialism and relate to men and women of other faiths. After all, was not faith a human quality which had to be taken seriously even when different expressions were used? No longer was it necessary to "protect" the gospel. Christ belonged to the world, to humanity and not just to the institutional churches.

But what about the absoluteness of Christ? For a long time the question returned — again and again. And there were times when the demands of loyalty to inherited affirmations led to excruciating agony, until I realized that the glorified Christ walks in and out of history and does not allow himself to be restricted by our interpretations. He makes himself known as the Unknown, eluding attempts to use him for the purpose of our own convenience. The Trinitarian dogma stood out against the background of an undifferentiated Absolute. The Christ in function was at once personal, impersonal and multi-personal and as a particular expression to me manifested in Jesus of Nazareth. Such an affirmation of Christ no more denied the uniqueness of Christ than knowledge of the fixed stars negated the sun.

At this stage of my journey I had become acquainted with Buddhism, particularly Zen. On the bench of the zendo I was firmly "educated down". The roshi's *keisaku* (stick) functioned like a sledge, demolishing attempts to give precedence to the rational faculty of the mind. I learned to breathe — one, two, three, four — and I noticed that many layers of my mind had been underdeveloped and neglected. I found that hitherto I had been preoccupied with all sorts of abstractions. How can I find God? What does the incarnation mean? Confronting myself in thoughts, distractions, fantasies and outcroppings of the unconscious proved clearly that a dimension of depth was sorely lacking. Images of God I knew, but I had almost no experience of the living God in me.

I remember the roshi saying: "You are a Christian, aren't you?" I answered quietly: "Yes, I hoped so." We sat on the veranda in front of the temple garden. I was painfully aware of the fact that he read my mind like an open book. He poked my chest twice saying: "God in you — that will be your koan!"

Two years of Zen training entirely changed my spiritual landscape. I was no longer desperately trying to affirm my own existence, my own standpoint, passing judgments and opinions about other people, about problems, not even about my eventual spiritual achievements. Some sort of basic trust whispered: you are not Atlas, the world is all there is, you are accepted. And when finally I left the Zen temple I felt like the person who was helped by the good Samaritan. Actually Buddhism acted like the good Samaritan, "bandaged (my) wounds, bathing them with oil and wine" (Luke 10:34).

Returning home I was delighted to discover previously hidden aspects of the Christian faith: the immense power of the Christian kerygma crystallized in a new way in Jesus the Christ. Theology was no longer isolated wisdom divorced from active verification in the soul. I had discovered a Christianity lost in Christendom, a wisdom lost in knowledge. The authoritarian image of God vanished. There was no longer any clear difference between the human self and the *imago Dei*.

When I look back on my spiritual journey I can't help thinking that my encounter with Zen-Buddhism was providentially prepared for me. I needed help to break through the self-centredness of a Western perspective. The Zen practice under the direction of the roshi firmly pointed out that so far I had mainly been engaged in cerebral exercises. And I said to myself that never again would I allow myself to become imprisoned in thinking about God, creating my own images about God and the world to come.

My previously somewhat unhappy relationship with the church was straightened out. First of all, I recognized that the church is an item of faith: I believe in one holy and catholic church. The church has a human face tainted with the usual weaknesses and shortcomings which belong to this world. Even more important was the realization that God addressed people in many different modes. Truth was given according to a person's capacity to comprehend, perhaps according to different spiritual temperaments. Persons in my local congregation were mainly farmers. Perhaps they had not had as much time to *think* about the matter as I had. I didn't have to decide the reason, but it seemed to me that most persons were unable to distinguish between truth and the forms in which it is dressed. I could understand the choice many Westerners are faced with. Either retaining their Absolute, which means absolutizing the forms in which Absolute truth comes to them: "In no other Name..."; or relativizing all forms, thus ending up in the standpoint of Frederik the Great: "Die Religionen müssen alle toleriert werden... denn hier muss ein jeder nach seiner Fasson seelig werden."

In my case I found that it was possible to retain a religious Absolute while gladly admitting the relativity of religious forms. I had discovered that any religious statement was simultaneously relative and absolute. Creeds and dogmas were transparent and made sense as provisional expressions of an absolute, transcendent Truth, unattainable and still immanently present. Thus I felt no need whatsoever to combat fundamentalism, but found that I had returned to my own tradition with a capacity to recognize that Truth is two-eyed, both absolute and relative.

My exposure to Buddhism made me painfully aware of the tragic impasse in the Western mentality. The challenge was to widen the Christian spectrum, allowing different aspects of the Christ event to speak to persons' varying inner needs. I had no wish at all to be critical of a child-like faith in God. How could I, since I knew well enough that such was the very basis of "my own" discovery. It seemed that God was calling us to let him act through new forms, or rather through forms which lay dormant within the Christian gospel itself. And I recognized that in my case the Buddhist way of reflection had introduced an understanding of the Christ event which was broad enough to cope with, yes, to resolve our modern predicament: the dichotomy of faith and reason, of being and substance, the personal and transcendent notions of God, the exaggerated role given to the knowing ego, and even the Judeo-Christian view of history itself. The transcendent God appeared as in St Augustine's well-known prayer: God, you are more close to me than my own heart.

Faith was not meant to be a weapon excluding others, but rather a joyful response to a transcendent and immanent calling. Such an understanding calls for a way of expressing Christian faith which is both absolute and relative. The positionless position of the living Christ needs to be made known today, hinting at the boundless horizon which alone can meet the human quest for life abounding. The Christ of no abode meets the longings of a modern person. As the Master said: "Foxes have their holes, the birds their roosts; but the Son of Man has nowhere to lay his head" (Luke 9:58).

It has been my joyful experience that the encounter between Buddhism and Christianity is one of the most meaningful events in the religious history of our time. Acting like the good Samaritan, Buddhism may help Christians to widen their perspectives, discovering that the Jesus way ultimately breaks through its own particularity accepting "other" expressions of the ultimate meaning of human existence as intrinsically grounded in the one cosmic and original fact of Immanuel (Gen. 9:9-16; John 1:1).

Still walking through the beautiful city of Kyoto or along the coastline of Öresund in my home country, Sweden, always I'll hear within myself reverberating with the beat of my heart: "God in you — that will be your koan!"

Integrating Other Religious Traditions into Western Christianity

ARNOLD BITTLINGER

The West-European Protestant tradition in which I was brought up is the foundation of my Christian spirituality. In the course of my life, this tradition has been supplemented and enriched by contact with Christians of other confessions and cultures, a particular influence being a growing familiarity with the liturgy and religious customs of the Orthodox Church.

In connection with my work in the field of charismatic renewal, ecumenical spirituality and depth psychology, I gradually got into contact also with non-Christian spiritual experiences and practices.

Since 1962 I have done research work on charismatic renewal. I have been a member of the core team in the dialogue between the Roman Catholic Church and Pentecostal/charismatic renewal movements.[1] I have also served as a consultant on charismatic renewal to the World Council of Churches.[2]

In the course of my research work I became interested in the African Independent churches[3], where I found a fine blend of traditional African and Christian elements. When I discovered that many charismatic elements in those churches had also roots in the African pre-Christian traditions I began to look for charismatic elements also in other religions. I discovered that especially the charismata of "healing" and of "prophecy" were sometimes more convincing in those religions than in the charismatic renewal — at least as far as it is influenced by the North American type of Christianity. In Shamanism I found fascinating parallels to the ministry of Jesus, whom I began to understand as an archetype of a Shaman.[4] Concerning "healing" I was especially impressed by the holistic approach to healing, which I found among American Indians. This motivated me to encourage such an approach also for our Christian healing services.

Concerning "prophecy" I am impressed by experiences in Hinduism. Some of our European "prophets" discovered and developed their prophetic gifts under the influence of Hindu gurus. Also other charismatic experiences have their sometimes very impressive equivalents in other religious traditions (e.g. "praying in the spirit" in Japa yoga). I am convinced that charismatic renewal will become more significant — especially for the mission of the church — if it also takes seriously the charismata of other religions.[5]

Since 1966 I have been involved in the work of an ecumenical academy[6] which is connected with an ecumenical community. A major concern of this work is the development of an ecumenical spirituality. But we are also interested in the spirituality of other religions. Thus, for example, we had a conference on the significance of Abraham as a root of faith in Judaism, Christianity and Islam[7] and a conference on African, Indian and Jewish spirituality with speakers of these traditions. We also had conferences on the Chinese I Ching and on the Tibetan Bardo Gödol. But our main concern is to go back to our own Celtic and Alemanic traditions and try to revitalize them in order to integrate them in our Christian belief. Thus we celebrate Solstice ("Sonnenwende") and the dark nights (24 December-6 January) where we pay special attention to our dreams. We also get acquainted anew with healing stones, waters, plants and places. We discover that under our Western European Christian surface there is still much "heathen" soil. Most Europeans have been "Christianized" in their mind, but their soul has never been converted to Christ. The famous Swiss psychologist Carl Gustav Jung writes:

> We must never forget our historical premises. Only a little more than a thousand years ago, we stumbled from the crudest beginnings of polytheism into the midst of a highly developed, oriental religion which lifted the imaginative minds of half-savages to a height which did not correspond to their degree of mental development. In order to keep to this height in some fashion or other, it was unavoidable that the sphere of the instincts was thoroughly repressed. Therefore, religious

practice and morality took on an outspokenly brutal, almost malicious character. The repressed elements are naturally not developed, but vegetate further in
the unconscious and in their original barbarism. [8]

And then Jung continues:

The development of Western intellect and will has lent us the almost devilish
capacity for imitating such an attitude, apparently with success too, despite the
protests of the unconscious. But it is only a matter of time when the counter
position forces recognition of itself with an even harsher contrast. [9]

These words of Jung were prophetic. A few years later, 1933-45, the
suppressed "heathen" spirit did break through (especially in Germany)
with such violence that after those years the heathen spirit, which had
behaved so badly, became suppressed even more. But this is of course a
false reaction, because the suppressed does not only "not develop", but it
remains a continuous threat — especially in the atomic age. Therefore we
try to bring again to consciousness our own pre-Christian roots and to
integrate them into the understanding of the cosmic Christ. This is for
instance done by integrating them into a Christian worship service or into
a Christian festival. We are convinced that such an integration is very
important — also for the survival of Christianity in Europe. I have met
American Indians and Africans who had left Christianity and gone back to
their old religious traditions, because these traditions were not integrated
in that type of Christianity into which their ancestors had been baptized. [10]
A similar process takes place in Europe.

I am also working as a psychotherapist. In psychotherapy again and again I
encounter in dreams and visions of Christians non-Christian symbols. Thus
one woman saw in her dream a turtle with a pillar on its back. I have seen this
very meaningful symbol [11] in East Asia, but never in Europe. I also encountered in dreams of people dragons as positive figures, which is strange to
Christianized Europe but very common in other traditions, especially in
Asia. Twice I met rather narrow-minded Christians who had (to their own
great astonishment!) positive dreams of the Buddha and thus became open
towards other religions and towards a larger view of Christianity.

In an ecumenical worship service a woman had the following vision:
she saw a cross in the Coptic style. At the top of this cross she saw a
European with a highly developed intellect. At the bottom of the cross she
saw an American Indian with his feet firmly grounded in mother earth. At
the right side she saw an African in vital and rythmic movement and at the
left side she saw an Asian in deep and silent meditation. The centre of the
cross (and thus the cross itself) was Christ:

European
(intellect)

Asian
(silence)

African
(movement)

American Indian
(earth)

This vision has — like other dreams and visions — a deep psychological meaning. It is a symbol of the individuation process, which encourages the "dreamer" to continue on her inner journey towards wholeness. But since this vision was seen in a worship service it also had a meaning for the church. It helped us to understand better the all-embracing lordship of the cosmic Christ.

Thus, inner psychic phenomena like dreams and visions point again and again to the values of other religions. Similarly many non-Christian religious symbols and practices point to the individuation process in our human soul. Thus the togetherness of a conscious and an unconscious "part" of the soul is demonstrated in many Shinto shrines by rocks which look out of a lake (or out of a "lake" of little stones). They point to the "visible" conscious and to the "invisible" unconscious. The unity of opposites, which is the heart of an individuation process, is beautifully symbolized by many Buddhist mandalas and by the Taoist symbol of yin and yang.

Some yoga practices have the same unifying effects as Western psychoanalysis. Many rebirth rituals in "primitive" religions are vivid images of the inner psychic process of dying and rising. More recently in analytical psychology a third level of the unconscious has been "discovered": the "empty" unconscious. [12] "Under" the personal and the collective unconscious there is still another level in which is "nothing" (and therefore everything!): the empty unconscious. I understand this "emptiness" in the deepest level of the human soul (which many Buddhists have experienced long before Western psychology "discovered" it!) as the level in which all human beings are connected with the cosmic Christ.

In our contact with other religions we find it helpful to consider three steps: (1) be firmly grounded in our own religious tradition and in the cultural tradition of our country; (2) try to understand other religious traditions and look especially for elements which are neglected in our own tradition; (3) carefully integrate those elements of other religious traditions which help us and our church to grow towards wholeness[13].

NOTES

[1] Cp. A. Bittlinger, *Papst und Pfingstler: Der römisch-katholisch-pfingstliche Dialog und seine öekumenische Relevanz*, Bern, 1978.

[2] Cp. A. Bittlinger ed., *The Church is Charismatic: the World Council of Churches and the Charismatic Renewal*, Geneva, WCC, 1981.

[3] Cp. A. Bittlinger *Afrikanische Christen*, Craheim, 1975.

[4] Cp. A. Bittlinger, *Schamanismus im Lichte der Bibel und der Psychotherapie*, Zürich, 1986. Cp. also "Recalling the Native Presence in Vancouver", *One World*, No. 100, November 1984.

[5] Cp. A. Bittlinger, "The Significance of Charismatic Experiences for the Mission of the Church", *International Review of Mission*, Vol. LXXV, No. 298, p. 117.

[6] Ökumenische Akademie im Nidelbad, cp. Directory of Study Centers, WCC/CWME, Geneva, 1982, p.60.

[7] The speeches are published in "Sammlung-Dienst-Sendung", Jg. 56, Nr. 3, Rüschlikon, 1980.

[8] R. Wilhelm and C.G. Jung, *The Secret of the Golden Flower*, London, 1931, p. 125.

[9] *Op. cit.*, pp. 126f.

[10] There are good examples of such an integration in some African Independent churches and also in some American Indian Native churches. Also in the beginning of Christianity the Greek Orthodox Church in Greece (!) and the Roman Catholic Church in Rome (!) have integrated well many elements of Greek and Roman pre-Christian traditions.

[11] The dreamer had of course no conscious knowledge of such a symbol.

[12] Cp. Peter Schellenbaum, *Abschied von der Selbstzerstörung*, Stuttgart, 1987, p. 186.

[13] I know only very few "Westerners" who are able to enter fully into another religious tradition, such as Hinduism or Zen Buddhism. For others such an attempt may even be harmful. Thus I am working with a person who has become schizophrenic by trying to become fully a Buddhist. In nearly every session he complains bitterly about his "stupidity" in trying to undertake such an effort. For many years I had close contact with a Western guru (Alfons Rosenberg) who also had tried in his younger years to enter fully into Indian religiosity. But he discovered that this was not possible for him as a Westerner. And thus he developed two Western forms of meditation: the cross-meditation and the labyrinth-meditation, because these two symbols have also deep roots in the Western culture.

Exploring Aboriginal Spirituality

COLIN ALCOCK

Unlike most other participants at this consultation I am not currently engaged in interfaith dialogue through contact with people of other faiths. However, since I expressed an interest in Zen spirituality, am associated with an institute concerned with Christian spirituality and was already in Kyoto for a consultation on peace, justice and the integrity of creation, I was invited to attend this consultation.

I am a founder and the executive director of Eremos (New Testament Greek "desert") Institute, an institute whose aims have been sloganized as "exploring Christian spirituality in our Australian context, and helping Christians understand and contribute to Australian society".

Though not being involved in active dialogue, it has become my conviction through the exploration of the riches of the Christian spiritual tradition that the relationship between different faiths is best understood in terms of their mystical/experiential traditions and that these traditions (as distinct from dogmatic expressions) will provide valuable insights into Christian faith and experience.

Through our exploration (which has included running ecumenical weekend retreats for lay and clergy, male and female, Christians and agnostics, plus through our seminars, publications and workshops) we have come more and more to the understanding that our Western context has fashioned our apprehension and experience of faith in radical ways, some of which have been unhelpful, not to say disastrous.

This understanding has had two major consequences. First, it has encouraged us all to become aware of the tentative character of our Western form of Christianity, enabling us a little more freedom to criticize both the church in our country and the values and meanings that seem to characterize our national life. And second, it has encouraged many of our members to express their exploration through contact with people of other faiths both in Australia and, most particularly, in India.

Some of these members gave up Christianity many years ago and have subsequently been on a search for spiritual meaning, others have simply become less enchanted by the older views that regard Christianity as the exclusive guardian of all truth.

In Eremos, people of both kinds have connected these experiences with a quest for a more realistic, informed and deeper way of experiencing their world and their God.

May I outline briefly the areas that are being addressed by Christians in Australia with regard to interfaith dialogue.

1. Over the past few years there has been an increasing interest in the spirituality of Aboriginal Australians. European settlement meant the devastation of Aboriginal traditions, community structures, and ways of being. It has, however, become more and more apparent that the Aboriginal Australians had developed a spirituality that was deeply attentive to this vast land. In stark contrast to Aboriginal societies, European settlers have for the most part hugged the rich coastal strips and avoided encounter with the harsh centre except where it could be materially exploited. Our attitude to the desert centre is, for many Christians, symbolic of an attitude to life that characterizes many in this land — the attempt to avoid whatever is deep, mysterious and possibly threatening, in an effort to remain secure and comfortable. In stark contrast to this, the Aboriginal people inhabited a numinous world where everything was charged with meaning and connected to everything else, a world where depth calls to depth. Within the Christian church today there is a concern to explore and appreciate Aboriginal perceptions of their relationship with the gods as part of our attempt to be at home in this place.

In an attempt to address this experientially, Eremos is planning to mount a programme which provides for small groups of people to go on expeditions to the Australian wilderness with the initial view to increasing our familiarity with the Australian desert and begin the process of "listening to the land". One of the leaders of this project was the former secretary for Aboriginal Affairs with the general synod of the Anglican Church in Australia. He will be particularly interested in connecting this project with Aboriginal communities in the "outback".

2. Like other Western countries, some popular and Westernized Eastern religions have won the allegiance of many younger people for whom the church was no longer seen as a "keeper of the dimension of depth". And so, yoga classes, Transcendental Meditation classes and, for the more serious, Hindu communes have had some degree of popularity. For the most part, the mainline churches seem to have either ignored or criticized these trends.

Eremos sponsored a visit to Australia by Dom Bede Griffith in 1985 and a number of our members have visited his ashram in South India. In Eremos we find that our appreciation of meditation and silence, along with our accepting attitude towards Eastern approaches to faith, has allowed us to begin to explore connections and enhance our understanding of the human quest for spiritual meaning.

Of Related Interest . . .

Orbis' Faith Meets Faith Series
in Interreligious Dialogue

Faith Meets Faith seeks to promote interreligious dialogue by providing
an open forum for exchanges between and among followers of different
religious paths. While the series wants to encourage creative and bold
responses to the new questions of pluralism confronting religious persons today, it also recognizes the present plurality of perspectives concerning the methods and content of interreligious dialogue.

THE CHALLENGE OF THE SCRIPTURES
The Bible and the Qur'ān
Muslim-Christian Research Group
Translated by Stuart E. Brown
Culminating a unique interfaith project, this book explores scripture as
a basis for Muslim-Christian dialogue. Islamic and Christian scholars
from Europe and North Africa, meeting independently over a period
of five years, begin by agreeing on the primacy of scripture, defining
and describing its role and meaning to Islam and to Christianity.

"A thorough and patient venture of mind and spirit which deserves to
be warmly welcomed and carefully weighed."
— **Bishop Kenneth Cragg**

ISBN 0-88344-650-2 Paper and 0-88344-651-0 Cloth
112pp. Index, appendix.

THE MEANING OF CHRIST
A Mahāyāna Theology
by John P. Keenan
A bold scholarly venture reinterpreting the Christian tradition in light
of Mahāyāna philosophy. Keenan uses Buddhist thought to unveil "fac-

ets of meaning in Christ not focused on in western thinking," to enable western Christian thinkers to reclaim their mystic tradition.

"A creative, pioneering work. ... The author's understanding also opens up new avenues of dialogue with and witness to Mahāyāna Buddhists."   —Ralph R. Covell

ISBN 0-88344-640-5 Paper and 0-88344-641-3 Cloth
300pp. Notes, bibliography, index.

HINDU-CHRISTIAN DIALOGUE
Perspectives and Encounters
Edited by Harold Coward
Foreword by Raimundo Panikkar
A unique anthology of the writings of eminent participants in Hindu-Christian dialogue covering topics and developments from the Hindus and the St. Thomas Christians (AD 52) to the present—and beyond.

"Covers the wide spectrum of the subject in an up-to-date way, and will be a very valuable resource for students, teachers, and the general reader."   —John Hick

ISBN 0-88344-633-2 Paper and 0-88344-634-0 Cloth
272pp. Index.

THE SILENCE OF GOD
The Answer of the Buddha
by Raimundo Panikkar
"Panikkar understands Buddhism with a depth that may surpass that of any other Christian. ... He is also genuinely a citizen of the modern or even post-modern world. This gives to his book an authority that must be acknowledged even by those who resist his interpretation."
—John B. Cobb, Jr.

ISBN 0-88344-445-3 Paper and 0-88344-446-1 Cloth
296pp. Notes, bibliography, indexes.

MANY PATHS
A Catholic Approach to Religious Pluralism
by Eugene Hillman
"Hillman, in the spirit of Vatican II, offers us this important book to

promote respect and openness among the great faiths of the world."

—John Macquarrie

ISBN 0-88344-548-4 Paper and 0-88344-547-6 Cloth
112pp. Notes, references, index.

LOVE MEETS WISDOM
A Christian Experience of Buddhism
by Aloysius Pieris
Within the framework of a pluralistic theology of religion, the Sri Lankan Jesuit explores the social as well as spiritual dimensions of Buddhism and issues pertinent to an interreligious understanding.

ISBN O-88344-371-6 Paper and 0-88344-372-4 Cloth
176pp. Notes, glossary, index.

THE DIALOGICAL IMPERATIVE
A Christian Reflection on Interfaith Encounter
by David Lochhead
Examines religious dialogue as relationships in social and historical context—and develops a theology of religion in a Barthian mode.

"An uncommonly wise and helpful book." —**Schubert M. Ogden**

ISBN 0-88344-611-1 Paper and 0-88344-612-X Cloth
112pp. Notes, index.

AN ASIAN THEOLOGY OF LIBERATION
by Aloysius Pieris
"It is the challenge of Aloysius Pieris that he seeks to trace the search for grace in Asian flesh and to articulate it in an Asian idiom. His voice deserves to be heard, his message pondered." —**William McConville**

ISBN 0-88344-626-X Paper and 0-88344-627-8 Cloth
160pp. Notes, bibliography, index.

THE MYTH OF CHRISTIAN UNIQUENESS
Toward A Pluralistic Theology of Religions
Edited by John Hick and Paul F. Knitter
A widely representative group of Christian theologians—including Wilfred Cantwell Smith, Rosemary Radford Ruether, and Raimundo

Panikkar—explores the meaning and consequences of pluralistic theology.

"An important study."   —David Tracy

ISBN 0-88344-602-2 Paper and 0-88344-603-0 Cloth
240pp. Notes, index.

TOWARD A UNIVERSAL THEOLOGY OF RELIGION
Edited by Leonard Swidler
Hans Küng, Wilfred Cantwell Smith, John Cobb, and Raimundo Panikkar dialogue with theologians of the major world religions.

"Urgently needed."   —Masao Abe

ISBN 0-88344-555-7 Paper and 0-88344-580-8 Cloth
264pp.